GARDENING
IN THE
SHADE

GARDENING IN THE SHADE

Alan Toogood

WARD LOCK

ACKNOWLEDGEMENTS

The publishers gratefully acknowledge the following agencies/photographers for granting permission to reproduce the colour photographs: Harry Smith Horticultural Photographic Collection (pp. 10, 11, 15, 34, 46, 59 & 86); Pat Brindley (pp. 30, 31, 42, 54, 75, 78 & 87); Peter McHoy (p. 47); and Photos Horticultural Picture Library (pp. 62, 63, 67, 82 & 83).

All the line drawings are by Nils Solberg.

First published in this edition in 1994
by Ward Lock, Villiers House, 41/47 Strand,
London WC2N 5JE, England

A Cassell Imprint

Originally published in the Concorde Gardening series in 1989

© Ward Lock 1989, 1994

Distributed in the United States by
Sterling Publishing Co., Inc.,
387 Park Avenue South, New York, NY 10016

Distributed in Australia by
Capricorn Link (Australia) Pty Ltd.,
2/13 Carrington Road, Castle Hill, NSW 2154

British Library Cataloguing in Publication Data
is available upon application to the British Library

ISBN 0 7063 7264 6

Text filmset in Bembo
by Hourds Typographica, Stafford
Printed and bound in Spain
by Cronion, S. A.

CONTENTS

CHAPTER 1

DEEP OR DAPPLED?

Shade in the garden is often considered a problem, where nothing will grow except perhaps a green carpet of moss. Actually, this can be a rather attractive feature in the dense shade of some large tree, but in fact moss is only one of a vast range of plants that will flourish in shade.

Shade should be regarded as an asset rather than a problem, for it enables one to grow a much wider range of plants than would be possible in a garden completely bathed in sunshine. There are true shade-lovers – those which grow under trees, etc, in their natural habitats. Many of these are charming, choice plants yet easy to grow given the right conditions in a garden.

Then there are plants which are very adaptable, growing and flowering equally well in sun or shade. You will soon discover how adaptable many plants can be by experimenting: if a particular plant appeals and you are unsure of the conditions it requires, then try it in shade. This is how many of our great gardeners and plantsmen have learned their art.

However, one should bear in mind that there is an equally wide range of plants which will not tolerate shade – these are the sun-lovers, coming from warm or hot, often dry places in the wild. The sun-lovers need really bright light and plenty of direct sun. Although they may survive in shade they will not grow and flower well. Often their stems become weak and spindly and their foliage pale.

At once I want to dispel the myth that shady gardens are dark, dull and uninteresting. No doubt this does apply in some instances; but the reason is that the owners have not chosen the right plants and have not included decorative features like statuary, mirrors and light-coloured paving materials to reflect light. Furthermore, the garden may be overgrown.

There are shade-loving plants suited to every part of the garden including, surprisingly, rock gardens and conservatories, and in general they are no more difficult to grow than those which need sun. Very dark corners can be considerably brightened, for example, with gold and silver variegated plants. It is simply not true that all of these plants have to be grown in sun. In my own garden the previous owners planted some golden conifers in an area which receives virtually no sun (only a little dappled sun first thing in the morning), yet they have retained a lot of their colour and considerably lighten this part of the garden. Even if they had reverted to pale green (as can happen with golden conifers in shade) they would still have the effect of lightening a dark area.

OBSERVING THE GARDEN

In order to decide where plants are to be grown we should first observe the garden over a period of time to determine which areas are in shade and which are sunny. We can then plant accordingly. There are various degrees of shade, each of which will support a different range of plants, so let us consider the types of shade that you may find in your garden.

VERY DEEP SHADE

Very deep shade – in other words, where the light intensity is very low and conditions are quite dark and gloomy – can be found under large trees with dense foliage, particularly evergreens (Fig. 1a), in the vicinity of large buildings and, of course, in basement gardens. Very often the soil is dry for much of the time in these situations. The roots of the trees extract most of the moisture from the soil, and the soil adjacent to walls and buildings can also be very dry, as the walls deflect rain.

This combination of deep shade and dry soil poses problems as few plants will grow in these conditions. There are some which will thrive, like hedera (ivies), ruscus (butcher's broom) and *Hypericum calycinum* (St. John's wort). However, these are not counted among the most attractive plants, although variegated ivies are not exactly dull plants and the hypericum is colourful when in flower.

Ideally one should try to let more light in if this is possible. This is only feasible, of course, where trees are creating the shade. A skilled tree surgeon should be able to thin out the canopy of branches, maintaining the tree's natural shape so that dappled shade is created (a combination of shade and sunlight). Then a much wider range of plants can be grown.

A dense group of trees will also create deep shade. In this instance the trees should be thinned out, so that there is space between them, and again the crowns thinned if necessary. It is surprising how much difference this will make to the range of plants that can be grown.

When I took over my present garden it was a dense jungle, having been neglected for years. A large part of the garden consisted of a dense 'stand' of young *Betula pendula* (silver birch). All the trees were growing into each other, with the branches intertwining, and conditions were very dark below when the trees were in leaf, with only bracken and brambles thriving.

Fig. 1 Types of shade. *(a)* Very deep shade can be found under large trees with dense foliage (such as beech), where the soil is also dry. In natural conditions moss often becomes established. *(b)* High walls, but with the area open to the sky, can result in light shade. *(c)* Dappled shade (a pattern of shade and sunlight) is found under deciduous trees with a light canopy of foliage, such as birches.

Well, I carried out a drastic thinning operation, resulting in light woodland with dappled shade; then I eradicated the bracken and brambles. What followed was quite amazing – wild digitalis (foxgloves) sprang up everywhere (as well as less desirable weeds!) and created a marvellous show of pink, purple and white spikes.

I am leaving large groups and drifts of these foxgloves, allowing them to perpetuate by self-seeding. But, of course, I now have the right conditions for many other woodland-type plants. Fortunately the soil is moist for much of the time, due to tree thinning and the accumulation of leafmould over the years.

If the soil is dry there are ways of helping to improve it, as discussed in Chapter 2. I should say that it is highly desirable to improve poor dry soil as much as possible, in order to be able to grow a wider range of plants.

A charming colony of candelabra primulas in the famous Hidcote garden in Gloucestershire. These lovely flowers will only flourish in cool, moist soil.

Being shallow-rooted shrubs, azaleas and other acid-loving woodlanders benefit from the shade of trees to prevent the soil drying out.

LIGHT SHADE

My interpretation here is the shade cast by walls, buildings, hedges and so on, but with the area open to the sky, so although there may be little or no sun the light is bright (Fig. 1b). The soil can also be dry in this situation, particularly immediately in front of walls and hedges. But, again, it is easily improved, as explained in Chapter 2.

A very wide range of attractive plants can be grown in light shade; and the walls can be clothed with colourful climbing plants and wall shrubs. There are even some roses which will grow on sunless (for example, north-facing) walls.

In a border with this type of shade there is no reason, of course, why some of the choice woodland-type plants should not be grown; and many of the ubiquitous but desirable shade-loving plants can share the border with them, such as the vast range of hostas, many primulas, ferns and the like.

DAPPLED SHADE

Many trees provide the most useful form of shade, particularly deciduous kinds (those which drop their leaves in the autumn) with a light canopy of foliage. It is popularly referred to as dappled shade because the foliage produces a pattern of shade and sunlight (Fig. 1c). Not all trees, though, produce this type of shade: those with very dense foliage, and the evergreens, can have quite deep shade beneath them.

In dappled shade a very wide range of plants can be grown, including woodland plants. In my opinion many of these are the most desirable and attractive plants we can grow in our gardens – what is more beautiful, say, than a group of candelabra primulas with their tiers of colourful flowers, and meconopsis (blue poppies) towering above a cool green tracery of ferns? Or, to herald the spring, drifts of *Primula vulgaris* (primrose) and galanthus (snowdrops)?

Most of these plants need moist soil as well as dappled shade. This is often found in light woodland, if the trees are well spaced. It is certainly the case in my own garden: although I am on sandy, well-drained soil the woodland area is blessed with deep deposits of leafmould, accumulated over the years, which help to retain soil moisture. As explained in Chapter 2, the addition of copious amounts of bulky organic matter like leafmould or peat, and perhaps the pruning and restriction of tree roots, will very much help in the retention of soil-moisture, thus allowing you to grow shade- and moisture-loving plants.

PARTIAL SHADE

This is rather a vague term, often used in gardening encyclopaedias and other text books, and invariably not explained. My interpretation of partial shade is an area of the garden which is shaded for part of the day and which receives full sun as well. For example, the area may be shaded by buildings in the morning, but sunny for the rest of the day. Partial shade, therefore, does not come within the scope of this book, for such areas receive enough sun for a very wide range of plants to be grown, including sun-lovers.

It is worth mentioning here those parts of the garden which receive early morning sun, as there are certain plants like camellias and magnolias which should not be grown in these conditions because their flower buds could be damaged or killed during frosty weather. This happens if frozen buds thaw out too quickly during early morning sunshine, so for these plants choose an area which is shaded in the morning so that frozen buds thaw out slowly.

HOW TO CREATE SHADE

There are gardens, of course – perhaps new ones or those in very open locations – which are sunny all day long, with only partial shade cast by the house. There is not much scope here for growing a collection of shade-loving plants unless one sets out to create more shady areas. This additional shade will result in a cooler, more restful and romantic garden. Although most of us like the sun, the glaring effect of an unshaded garden can be rather uncomfortable all day long. A combination of sunny and shady areas also gives a garden character and an air of mystery.

CHOOSING TREES
I indicated earlier that deciduous trees with a light canopy of foliage provide the best type of shade (dappled), so if space permits I suggest planting a few trees – even a small group to create a mini-woodland. There are several fairly small-growing kinds suitable for all but the small 'pocket-handkerchief' garden.

Most people will plant trees as single specimens, perhaps having several if space permits. If you want to plant a group of trees to form a mini-woodland it generally looks better to stick to just one kind, such as a group of betula (birches) or malus (apples and crab apples).

In either case you will want some idea of the ultimate spread of the trees. Here we come to a difficult aspect because the spread of a tree depends upon its surroundings. For example, the branches of trees which are growing very close together, or which are surrounded by tall buildings, tend to grow upright with very little outward spread. But trees with plenty of space around them will spread more.

To give some idea, though, one can assume that the ultimate spread will be approximately 40% of the final height. When planting groups of trees one should allow more than this – say 50% of the ultimate height – to ensure there is still space between the trees at maturity.

In the following choice of trees I have quoted the ultimate height for each. Please note, however, that I am not considering fastigiate kinds (those with a slim habit whose branches naturally grow erect) as they do not provide much in the way of shade, and spreads are not a problem anyway.

Several of the acers (maples) provide the type of shade we desire, including *Acer capillipes* (snake-bark maple) with very attractive bark: it is green, finely striped with white. The new twigs are conspicuous, too, being bright red. In the autumn the leaves turn red – a spectacular sight. Height 9 m (30 ft). A very popular tree is *A. negundo* 'Variegatum' (the variegated box elder), with green and white variegated foliage. Height 9 m (30 ft). Both of these trees are generally grown as single specimens.

Excellent for forming groups are species of betula (birch). Their one drawback is that the roots grow just below the surface of the soil and spread quite widely, so the ground can be dry underneath. *B. pendula* (common silver birch) is native to Britain and has a very dainty, light crown and white bark. Height 15–18 m (50–60 ft). The Chinese species *B. albo-sinensis septentrionalis* has conspicuous orangy-brown bark – an attractive feature in the winter garden. Height 18 m (60 ft).

Crataegus (thorns), either alone or in groups, are excellent shade trees for small gardens. *C. monogyna* 'Biflora' (Glastonbury thorn) is a variety of the common hawthorn, with fragrant white flowers in the spring and another 'flush' in the winter when the weather is mild. Height 6 m (20 ft). Also recommended is *C.* × *prunifolia*, with white flowers in spring followed by red fruits. The autumn leaf colour is superb – brilliant shades of red and orange. Height 6 m (20 ft).

Malus (apples and crab apples) are highly recommended, too. Apples are traditional shade trees of English cottage gardens and old specimens have a charming character all their own.

There are quite a few ornamental crab apples and a universal favourite is *M. floribunda*. This Japanese species is at its most spectacular in spring when the light pink flowers emerge from bright red buds. These are followed in the autumn by yellow crab apples. Height 6–9 m (20–30 ft). Apples, and indeed crab apples, can be grown in groups, of course, if you wish to shade a large area. Bear in mind that these days they are often sold on dwarfing rootstocks which produce small trees. These are not really ideal for our purpose so choose specimens on more vigorous root-stocks to ensure larger trees.

The much-prized blue Himalayan poppy, *Meconopsis betonicifolia*, is another plant that insists on a cool moist spot shaded by trees from the summer sun.

Another tree of great character, traditionally grown for shade and fruits in English cottage gardens, is *Morus nigra* (black mulberry). This produces deep red, juicy, rather acid fruits. It is somewhat fussy regarding conditions, needing a deep, moist, fertile soil and a site which is sheltered from cold winds. Best results in milder parts of the country. It is quite a spreading tree: the width can almost equal the height, which is 6–9 m (20–30 ft).

Prunus (ornamental cherries, etc) offer many species and varieties for small gardens. I will simply suggest two of my favourites, both performing when most others are at their dullest. *P. sargentiana* is famed for its spectacular autumn leaf colour – shades of red and orange. Pink flowers appear in early spring amidst the unfurling bronzy leaves. Height 15 m (50 ft). *P. subhirtella* 'Autumnalis' (the autumn cherry) produces its small semi-double white flowers during mild spells in autumn and winter. Height 6–9 m (20–30 ft). Both of these prunus look superb when planted in a woodland garden, with other trees such as birches. Equally suitable for mixed borders. Both need a dark background to show them off. For instance, the flowers of the autumn cherry show up well against a background of tall deep green evergreen shrubs.

Sorbus species are attractive and useful trees for small gardens, having a dainty canopy of foliage. *S. aucuparia* (mountain ash or rowan) grows wild in Britain and in spring is clothed with white flowers while in autumn, birds permitting, it is bedecked with bunches of reddish-orange berries. Height 12–15 m (40–50 ft). The Chinese *S. hupehensis* can also be recommended. It has white flowers in spring and these are followed by white or pink berries. The leaves take on brilliant red or orange tints in the autumn. Height 12 m (40 ft). The sorbus look good planted in groups, space permitting, or may be grown as single specimens, such as in a mixed border.

PERGOLA WITH CLIMBERS

Of course, trees take time to grow and it will therefore be several years before they start producing a reasonable amount of shade. Quicker results can be achieved by erecting a timber pergola and training climbing plants over it.

Part of a patio could be covered with a pergola and in small beds below it a collection of shade-loving plants can be grown (Fig. 2). Pergolas are also often erected over garden paths and in this instance the plants could be grown in narrow borders on each side of the path.

These days pergolas are available in kit form and are very easy to erect.

Obviously you should choose some reasonably quick-growing climbing plants for training over the pergola. They can, of course, be sun-

Fig. 2 A timber pergola over part of a patio, with a climber trained over it such as the ornamental vine, *Vitis* 'Brant', will provide dappled shade under which various plants will flourish.

loving plants as their heads will be in the sun. Possibly one of the best is an ornamental grape vine with edible fruits: *Vitis* 'Brant'. The large hand-like leaves result in dappled shade and take on colourful tints in the autumn. The black grapes can be used for wine-making if desired. Climbing roses and clematis are suitable and make marvellous companions. Allow them to intertwine. Lonicera (honeysuckles) and jasminum (jasmines) are suitable too.

For something rather different why not have a laburnum arch over a path? I know that laburnum is a tree, but it is very amenable to training and in fact can be trained over an arch or pergola, when the yellow flowers will hang down inside during late spring and early summer. The best type of support for laburnum is a metal pergola with rounded arches. The steel arches are set 2 m (6 ft) apart and linked together with heavy duty galavanized wire. Obtain laburnum bushes rather than young trees as these will produce several stems from ground level, and plant them 3 m (10 ft) apart on either side of the pergola. Stems are spaced out and tied in to the wires, which should be 60 cm (2 ft) apart. Each year the side shoots that are produced on the main stems or branches are cut back to two or three buds. This is done in early winter. Suitable laburnums for such training are *L. alpinum, L. anagyroides* and *L. × watereri* 'Vossii' (the latter has ultra-long trusses of flowers). Bear in mind that all parts of laburnum are poisonous.

HEDGES AND SCREENS

To create an element of surprise a garden can be divided into a number of smaller areas – what I like to call 'secret gardens'. The divisions can be made with hedges, either formal or informal; with walls, such as the popular screen-block walling; with timber trellis panels; or, more informally, with groups of tall shrubs. Hedges and screens will have a shady side if they are suitably positioned and so a well-divided garden should have plenty of shady beds or borders. The north side of a hedge or screen will be the shady side.

Climbing plants can be grown up screens formed of timber trellis panels or screen-block walling.

Large shrubs and small trees planted within these 'secret gardens' will all help to provide shady spots. But do not overdo such planting, otherwise it is possible you will create a gloomy garden. Aim for a good balance between shady and sunny areas and then you will be able to grow all kinds of plants and have a garden of contrasts and surprises.

CHAPTER 2

THE GROUNDWORK

It is often necessary to improve the soil in shady parts of the garden, as roots of trees (especially large forest types such as fagus or beeches) can extract most of the moisture and nutrients. The soil in front of hedges is often poor and dry, for the same reason; and often the ground is dry in front of walls, due to rain being deflected away from them.

Thorough soil preparation prior to planting is often necessary if plants are to thrive. Aftercare of plants should not be neglected either: often they need more watering and feeding than plants in other parts of the garden, and in dry conditions mulching is especially important for it helps to prevent moisture evaporating from the upper layer of soil.

SOIL IMPROVEMENT

If you are faced with dry soil under trees or in front of walls you should dig in copious amounts of bulky organic matter, which acts like a sponge and helps to retain moisture. It can be incorporated during digging, ideally deep digging to two depths of the spade blade (known as double digging) (Fig. 3). A layer of organic matter is spread in the bottom of each trench. As a guide, about a quarter of a wheelbarrow-load to each

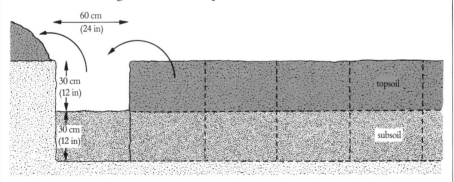

Fig. 3 Difficult soil can be improved by double digging and incorporating large amounts of bulky organic matter in each trench. This technique is especially recommended for very dry soils. The subsoil (the lower level) is well broken up to the depth of a fork.

1.2 m (4 ft) length of trench. Also mix organic matter into the top 30 cm (12 in) of soil, either during or after digging.

Suitable types of organic matter include well-rotted garden compost, leafmould, peat, pulverized bark, spent mushroom compost (not for lime-hating plants as it contains chalk), and spent hops.

Finally, lightly fork into the soil surface a dressing of slow-release organic fertilizer, such as blood, fish and bone.

You cannot do anything about tree roots immediately under trees, but you can stop them spreading into nearby beds and borders, say just beyond the branch spread; and you can also prevent the roots of hedges penetrating borders. Such root control will very much help to prevent beds and borders becoming dry and short of nutrients.

Firstly, cut the roots back and remove them. Then dig a trench about 75 cm (2½ ft) deep and line it with thick polythene sheeting, with the top edge just below ground level. Finally, fill in the trench with soil. Such a trench can be about 90 cm (3 ft) away from a hedge. The roots will not grow through the polythene, but will certainly grow in another direction in search of moisture and nutrients; but hopefully where they will not interfere with other plants!

If the soil is naturally moist in the shady area, preparations prior to planting should be a bit easier. I still advocate thorough digging of the bed or border and, unless the soil is naturally rich in humus (such as leaf-mould) it is a good idea to dig in peat, leafmould or pulverized bark, for many of the plants we grow in shade are woodlanders and appreciate the humus provided by these materials. Again, apply a dressing of slow-release organic fertilizer before planting.

PERNICIOUS WEEDS

If one has taken over a neglected garden, or indeed a new plot, one may be faced with pernicious perennial weeds. I was when I took over my garden, which had been neglected for many years. The ground beneath the trees was a tangle of brambles, bracken and ground elder.

It is best to eradicate such weeds before digging commences. I sprayed my tangled undergrowth several times during the growing season with a weedkiller containing glyphosate. This did the trick: by the end of the growing season the undergrowth was dead. I then commenced digging, removing the roots of the weeds as I proceeded. I have had no trouble since: apart from seedling weeds.

Glyphosate, which is perfectly safe to use, has to be applied with precision and in suitable weather conditions, when weeds are in full growth, so it is vital to follow the maker's instructions on use (as, indeed, it is with any chemical).

PLANTING

Deeply dug soil should be firmed before planting by treading it sysematically with your heels. If this is not done the soil will sink at a later date and the ground may end up uneven.

If you are planting in poor dry soil I would highly recommend the use of a proprietary planting mixture, as this gets plants off to a good start. Basically, it consists of peat with added fertilizers, often formulated for different types of plants, such as shrubs or perennials.

After making the planting hole you add some planting mixture to the bottom and fork it in. You also add some of the mixture to the soil which is to be returned over the roots and around the plant. Then you plant in the normal way.

You can, if you wish, make up your own planting mixture, such as a large bucketful of moist peat with a small handful of slow-release organic fertilizer mixed well in, such as sterilized bonemeal, hoof and horn meal, or blood, fish and bone.

If you are planting climbing plants against a wall, or alongside a tree trunk with the intention of allowing the climber to grow up into the tree, do not plant closer than 30 cm (12 in), otherwise the plant could suffer from dryness at the roots and be slow to establish, or fail altogether. The stems should be guided to their support by means of bamboo canes angled towards the wall or trunk (Fig. 4).

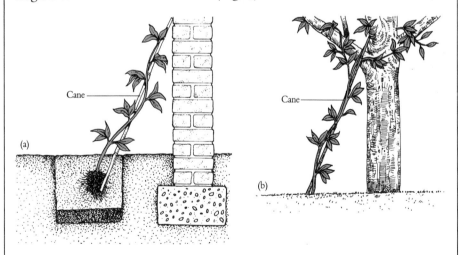

Fig. 4 Climbers should not be planted hard up against a wall or tree where the soil is generally very dry, but rather at least 30 cm (12 in) away from the support, with bamboo canes angled towards it.

A word about planting steep banks (see Chapter 5). When I tackled my bank I decided it was best not to dig the soil for fear of loosening it too much, which could have resulted in movement. So I simply eradicated the perennial weeds with glyphosate and then planted in well-prepared holes, as described above. The planting mixture got the plants off to a really good start and they have never looked back. They are now growing together well, so stabilizing the loose, sandy soil.

AFTERCARE OF PLANTS

Some plants growing in shade, particularly dry shade, will need a bit more attention than normal, especially when it comes to watering and feeding. Mulching is important in dry shade and this can also help in the other aspect of care – weed control.

WATERING

This will be an important task in areas where the soil dries out rapidly due to tree or hedge roots; also immediately in front of walls where rain does not reach. It is especially important not to allow newly planted subjects to dry out. Once established, some plants are able to cope more easily with dry conditions.

In dry parts of the garden it may, perhaps, be a good idea to install some permanent water sprinklers, such as the pop-up type, so that the plants can be watered simply at the turn of a tap. Or perforated irrigation tubing could be laid between plants, simply needing a hosepipe connected to it whenever watering is required.

It goes without saying that you need to apply adequate water to ensure it penetrates to a reasonable depth. A 'quick splash' with a hosepipe will do no good at all. The aim should be to keep the top 15 cm (6 in) moist, which means applying water when the top 2.5 cm (1 in) of the soil surface starts to become dry.

One must apply sufficient water for it to penetrate at least 15 cm (6 in) deep and this means the equivalent of 2.5 cm (1 in) of rain. This amounts to approximately 27 litres of water per sq m ($4\frac{3}{4}$ gallons per sq yd). To apply this amount it makes sense to use a sprinkler of some kind.

You can measure the amount of water being applied by standing a few empty tin cans over the area. When these have 2.5 cm (1 in) of water in the bottom you know that sufficient water has been applied. However, I consider it a good idea to check the depth of penetration about an hour after watering, by digging a 15 cm (6 in) deep test hole with a hand trowel. If the soil is moist at the bottom you know that sufficient water has been applied. (Don't forget that in the UK you have to pay a fee to the local water authority for the use of a garden sprinkler.)

FEEDING

All garden plants need feeding regularly, at least once a year, and this certainly applies to shade plants which are growing in the vicinity of tree roots, where nutrients are quickly depleted. A mid- or late spring feed is recommended, with perhaps another in the summer.

Any proprietary flower-garden fertilizer can be used, but I am quite keen on the slow-release organic blood, fish and bone, which releases its foods over a period of time.

Fertilizer should be sprinkled evenly around the plants, at the rate recommended by the manufacturer, and then lightly forked or hoed into the surface. If the soil is dry the fertilizer should also be watered in. If the ground is mulched (see below) the mulching material is best drawn away from around the plants to expose the soil before applying fertilizer. When the fertilizer has been added, the mulch is spread back around the plants.

MULCHING

This is a technique whereby the soil between plants is permanently covered with a layer of bulky organic matter. It helps to conserve soil moisture during dry periods (it prevents moisture evaporating from the surface) and will suppress the growth of weed seeds.

The most attractive-looking mulching materials for the ornamental parts of the garden are peat, leafmould and shredded or pulverized bark, either chipped or partially composted bark. Bark is the longest-lasting material. If you manage to collect sufficient leaves each autumn you can, of course, make your own leafmould. Oak and beech leaves are the best but they are slow to rot down – they take two years. Moist leaves are stacked in a heap in the autumn and then you simply wait until they have decomposed into a dark brown, crumbly material.

Garden compost is an excellent mulching material too, but possibly not as attractive in appearance as the above materials. The same comments apply to well-rotted farmyard manure.

Lay the mulching material evenly to a depth of 5–7.5 cm (2–3 in) in the spring. The soil should be completely free from weeds and moist. Prior to laying the mulch, apply a dressing of fertilizer. Check the mulch annually and top it up if necessary.

WEEDING

If you eradicated perennial weeds prior to planting, you should only be troubled by seedling weeds, mainly annual kinds, but also perennials as there are bound to be large numbers of their seeds still in the soil. In my garden I get bramble seedlings springing up everywhere.

There are various ways of controlling seedling weeds which, of course, are a problem in soil that has not been mulched. Hoeing regularly while the weeds are still small is the traditional way. Choose a warm, dry breezy day when the soil surface is dry and the weeds will quickly shrivel and die.

Weeds can also be controlled among plants by spraying them with a weedkiller containing paraquat, but on no account get this on the leaves of cultivated plants or it will kill the foliage and maybe the entire plant. Paraquat is especially useful around larger woody plants such as shrubs.

It is possible to keep the soil free from seedling weeds by using a weed-killer containing propachlor. This prevents the germination of seeds and is effective for a period of up to eight weeks. This weedkiller will not harm any plants and is applied as granules from a shaker pack. These should be applied evenly to moist weed-free soil. Follow the manufacturer's instructions on use. After application the soil must not be disturbed in any way.

If the odd perennial weed appears among plants treat it with a 'spot-weeder' containing glyphosate. But make sure this weedkiller does not come into contact with cultivated plants.

CHAPTER 3

THE MIXED BORDER

The mixed border is invariably the major feature of modern gardens. All kinds of plants are grown together but the 'framework' is generally formed of shrubs. Around the shrubs, contrasting and blending with them in colour, texture and shape, are other kinds of plant such as hardy perennials and bulbs.

A well-planned mixed border should provide colour and interest throughout the year.

Generally it is recommended that a mixed border is sited in a sunny position but this is not always possible. Nevertheless there are many shrubs, perennials and bulbs which can be grown in a shady border. I am thinking of a border in light shade, with the area open to the sky, so although there may be little or no sun the light is bright.

PLANNING THE BORDER

There are many ways of planning a mixed border. For example, one could aim for the major display to take place during a particular season – say spring or summer, or it could really come to life in the autumn with foliage tints and berries. This idea means that the border will be dull for much of the year and therefore is not generally recommended, but it's a thought for those people who spend a lot of time away from home, or who own, say, a holiday cottage. In these instances the border could be planned to provide the most colour while the owners are in residence.

However, most people will want to spread colour and interest over all four seasons, with parts of the border in turn providing the show. I rather like the idea of planting seasonal groups of plants so that bold effects are achieved.

For instance, a spring group could contain as a 'centrepiece' a *Magnolia* × *soulangiana* with its white, purple-flushed flowers. Around this shrub you could have a carpet of bergenias with pink or purplish blooms and bold evergreen foliage. Small narcissus (daffodils) could be allowed to grow through the bergenias, or be drifted around them. A perfect spring picture (Fig. 5).

A summer group could feature lacecap hydrangeas such as 'Blue

Wave'. If you have dappled shade from a small tree this would be an ideal spot for these shrubs. Marvellous companions for hydrangeas are the hostas (plantain lilies) with their large, bold leaves which contrast beautifully with hydrangeas in shape, colour and texture. Further contrast could be provided with groups of *Galtonia candicans* (summer hyacinth), with its spikes of white flowers and strap-shaped foliage (Fig. 6).

I love planning groups for autumn colour, using plants with fiery foliage, colourful berries and flowers. As a centrepiece try *Euonymus europaeus* 'Red Cascade' whose leaves take on red tints in autumn, when the shrub is laden with pinky-red fruits. Flowering in autumn is the hardy perennial *Anemone × hybrida* so this could be drifted around the euonymus, perhaps choosing a white variety for contrast. Colchicums (autumn crocuses), with pink, mauve, purple or white crocus-like flowers would complete the picture.

Winter groups are equally exciting, I feel, and one of my favourite shrubs for this period is *Cornus alba* 'Sibirica' with brilliant crimson stems. These show up well against a background of *Mahonia japonica*

Fig. 5 A spring group in a mixed border. The shrub is *Magnolia ×　soulangiana* while around it are planted bergenias with their bold evergreen foliage and purplish blooms, and groups of yellow daffodils.

Fig. 6 A summer group in a mixed border. This features a group of lacecap hydrangea 'Blue Wave', surrounded by hostas with bold leaves, and groups of *Galtonia candicans* (summer hyacinth) with spikes of white flowers.

with its shiny deep green foliage and sprays of scented yellow flowers. Complete the picture with some clumps of *Helleborus orientalis* (Lenten rose), with pink, purple, red or white flowers in late winter/early spring. Among the Lenten roses could nestle groups of *Galanthus nivalis* (snowdrops).

Alternatively, you could plan groups to provide a succession of colour so that at any one time there is something colourful or interesting. Of course, there are countless combinations, so let me give one example of how to plan part of a border for successional colour.

We need plants for each season, so for spring why not consider *Pieris formosa* 'Forrestii' (provided you have acid or lime-free soil), with white flowers and eye-catching bright red young leaves. Around this you could have drifts of the blue *Muscari armeniacum* (grape hyacinth). The shrub *Leycesteria formosa* could provide the summer colour. It has white flowers but more showy are the wine-red bracts that surround them. I suggest a white border phlox, *P. paniculata*, as a companion. Autumn could be heralded with the red berries of *Viburnum opulus* (guelder rose), underplanted with colchicums (autumn crocuses). For winter, a universally favourite shrub: *Hamamelis mollis* with spidery yellow flowers on bare branches, surrounded with a drift of *Helleborus orientalis* (Lenten rose).

I hope these few examples will give you an idea of how to plan a shady mixed border. Let us now take a more detailed look at a range of shrubs, perennials and bulbs that would be suitable for these conditions.

A CHOICE OF PLANTS

SHRUBS

Cornus (dogwood)

Cornus alba and its varieties are noted for their red stems, which show up particularly well in winter. One of the best varieties is *C. a.* 'Sibirica' (the Westonbirt dogwood), with brilliant crimson stems. Varieties with variegated leaves help to lighten a shady border, like white and green 'Elegantissima' and yellow and green 'Spaethii'. Each year in early spring cut stems down to within a few centimetres of the ground. Cornus like moist soil. Height and spread 2.4 m (8 ft).

Corylopsis

The spring-flowering *Corylopsis pauciflora* bears scented, light yellow flowers on bare twigs. Height and spread at least 1.8 m (6 ft). Best in acid soil, although succeeds in alkaline conditions provided the soil contains plenty of humus. Try to find a sheltered position for this shrub, as it hates cold winds.

Daphne

Several species are excellent for shade, including *D. mezereum* (mezereon), a deciduous shrub which flowers in winter and spring. Flowers may be pink, purple or white. Height 1.5 m (5 ft), spread up to 1.2 m (4 ft). *D. × burkwoodii* is partially evergreen and bears pink flowers in spring/early summer. A good variety is 'Somerset'. Height and spread 1.2 m (4 ft).

Euonymus (spindle tree)

Two species for autumn colour can be recommended. *E. europaeus* 'Red Cascade' is laden in autumn with pinky-red fruits and the leaves take on red tints. Height and spread up to 3 m (10 ft). *E. alatus* has unusual 'winged' branches, and in autumn red foliage and purplish fruits. Height and spread at least 2.4 m (8 ft).

Fothergilla

These deciduous shrubs have white bottle-brush-like flowers in spring. The best-known is *F. monticola* whose foliage turns to shades of orange and red in autumn. Height and spread at least 2.4 m (8 ft). Must be grown in acid soil which is able to retain moisture and has a plentiful supply of humus.

Hamamelis (witch hazel)
Deciduous shrubs flowering in winter. One of the most popular is *H. mollis* 'Pallida' with light yellow blooms. All witch hazels have spidery flowers. Another good variety is *H. m.* 'Goldcrest' with golden-yellow blooms. Height and spread in excess of 2.4 m (8 ft). Provide a soil rich in humus which is moisture-retentive.

Hydrangea
Hydrangeas thrive in a sheltered site with moist soil and flower for a long period in the summer, often into autumn. Avoid a site which receives early morning sun as frozen flower buds could be damaged. *H. sargentiana* is a large shrub, height and spread about 3 m (10 ft), and has flat heads of pink and white flowers set against deep green leaves. *H. villosa* is of similar stature and bears light purple and white flowers. *H. macrophylla* offers some attractive varieties, especially *H. m. serrata* 'Grayswood' with blue and white flowers, height and spread at least 1 m (3 ft). The lacecap group of *H. macrophylla* has attractive flat heads of flowers, blue in the variety 'Blue Wave' (or pink in alkaline soils). Height and spread 1.2– 1.8 m (4–6 ft).

Leycesteria
The green-stemmed *L. formosa* sports white flowers surrounded by wine-red bracts in the summer, followed by deep purple fruits. Height and spread 1.8 m (6 ft). Each year in early spring prune out completely stems which flowered the previous year.

Magnolia
This is a large and diverse genus, but for the mixed border choose the shrubby species which flower at an early age, like the universally popular *M.* × *soulangiana* or its varieties with huge white cup-shaped flowers, flushed with purple, in the spring, before the leaves appear. Height and spread at least 4.5 m (15 ft). *M. stellata* has white star-shaped flowers in early spring, before the leaves. Height and spread at least 2.4 m (8 ft), but slow-growing. Choose a position sheltered from cold winds and avoid early morning sun.

Mahonia
These evergreen shrubs have bold, attractive foliage and large heads of yellow flowers. Plant them in cool, moist, peaty soil. A favourite species

is *M. japonica* which has delightfully fragrant flowers in winter and spring. Height and spread at least 2.4 m (8 ft). The hybrid *M.* × 'Charity' is also widely grown, of similar stature, and also with fragrant flowers which appear between late autumn and late winter.

Paeonia (peony)
This genus contains both shrubs and herbaceous perennials. Of the shrubby kinds, *P. lutea ludlowii* thrives in light shade. Deciduous, with scented yellow flowers in early summer. Height and spread up to 1.8 m (6 ft). Avoid a position which receives early morning sun. Best in moist, humus-rich soil.

There is no need to look upon shady ground as a problem when honesty (*Lunaria biennis*) and green *Helleborus corsicus* will thrive there.

Pieris

The pieris are among the most attractive evergreen shrubs for acid soils and are equally at home in the dappled shade of a woodland garden. They like a moist, humus-rich soil and shelter from cold winds. Pieris flower in the spring and bear trusses of white bell-shaped flowers. There are several species, including *P. floribunda*, height and spread 1.8 m (6 ft); *P. formosa*, of which the variety 'Forrestii' is recommended, with bright red young leaves in the spring, height and spread up to 3.6 m (12 ft); *P.* 'Forest Flame', whose new foliage is bright red, turning pink, cream and finally green, height and spread up to 3 m (10 ft); and *P. japonica*, height and spread up to 3 m (10 ft), of which I recommend the varieties 'Blush'

Many of the daintier spring-flowering bulbs, narcissus and the variously coloured forms of *Anemone blanda* among them, bloom happily in light shade.

with palest pink flowers, the pure white 'Purity', and 'Variegata' with cream-edged leaves.

Skimmia

Small evergreen shrubs with heads of white flowers in spring and red berries in autumn/winter. There are separate male and female plants, the latter bearing the berries. The best-known species is *S. japonica*, height and spread 1.5–1.8 m (5–6 ft). There are several varieties: 'Foremanii' (female), 'Fragrans' (male, with highly scented flowers), 'Nymans' (female, large fruits), and 'Rubella' (male, with conspicuous red flower buds in winter). Plant both male and female plants for berries. *S. reevesiana* is hermaphrodite and bears crimson berries. Height and spread 1 m (3 ft).

Stachyurus

Deciduous shrubs, flowering in spring. *S. praecox* has pendulous trusses of light yellow flowers which are borne on bare branches, making them more obvious. Choose a sheltered spot with humus-rich soil. Height and spread 3 m (10 ft).

Stranvaesia

The evergreen cotoneaster-like *S. davidiana* has white flowers in early summer and red berries in autumn (or yellow in variety 'Flava'). Height and spread at least 6 m (20 ft).

Symphoricarpos (snowberry)

Deciduous shrubs noted for white or pink berries in autumn. Suitable for quite deep shade and dry soil. *S. albus* 'Laevigatus', height and spread at least 1.8 m (6 ft), has large white berries. *S. orbiculatus*, similar stature, bears purplish or pink berries.

Viburnum

A large genus of deciduous and evergreen shrubs. Popular species for mixed borders include *V. farreri* (syn. *V. fragrans*), deciduous, winter flowering, scented, white, pink-flushed blooms, height and spread at least 3 m (10 ft). *V.* × *bodnantense* 'Dawn', deciduous, winter flowering, scented white flowers, tinted pink, height and spread up to 3.6 m (12 ft). *V. opulus* 'Notcutts Variety', deciduous, white flowers early summer, red berries autumn, also autumn leaf colour, height and spread 3.6 m (12 ft). *V.* × *burkwoodii*, evergreen, fragrant white flowers in spring, height and spread about 2.4 m (8 ft). Provide a moisture-retentive soil, shelter from cold winds and avoid early morning sun.

PERENNIALS

Aconitum (monkshood)

Herbaceous perennials with spikes of hooded flowers in summer. Plants are poisonous. *A. napellus* varieties are recommended, especially 'Bressingham Spire' with dark violet-blue flowers, height 90 cm (3 ft), spread 30 cm (12 in). Provide moist soil.

Anemone (windflower)

A. × *hybrida* (syn. *A. japonica, A.* × *elegans*) flowers in late summer and autumn. Height 60–90 cm (2–3 ft), spread 30–45 cm (12–18 in). Varieties come in shades of pink and also white. The latter show up especially well in shade. Leave undisturbed once planted.

Aquilegia (columbine)

Herbaceous plants with attractive ferny foliage and showy, spurred flowers. *A. vulgaris* 'McKana Hybrids' come in a wide range of colours and flower during early summer. Height 90 cm (3 ft), spread 30 cm (12 in). Grow in moist, humus-rich soil.

Astrantia (masterwort)

Herbaceous plants with starry flowers in summer. *A. major* is a well-known species with pinkish-green flowers. Height 60 cm (2 ft), spread 30 cm (12 in). *A. carniolica* 'Rubra', 30 cm high, has reddish-purple flowers.

Bergenia

Evergreen perennials valued perhaps less for their flowers than for their large leathery leaves, which sometimes become tinted red or purple in winter. *B. cordifolia* is well-known, with heads of mauve-pink flowers in spring. *B. c. purpurea* has purple-flushed foliage. Height and spread 30 cm (12 in). *B. crassifolia*, of similar stature, has light pink blooms in winter and spring. Similar is *B. purpurascens*, flowering in spring. 'Ballawley' is a good variety with red flowers. *B. stracheyi* has some good varieties, especially the white 'Silberlicht' ('Silver Light'), flowering in spring, height and spread 30 cm (12 in).

Campanula (bellflower)

A very large and diverse genus. Popular mixed-border species, herbaceous in habit, include *C. lactiflora* with pale blue bells on branching stems in summer. A good form is 'Prichard's Variety', dark blue. Height 90 cm (3 ft), spread 45 cm (18 in). *C. persicifolia* (the peach-leaved bellflower), has cup-shaped blue or white flowers on 90 cm (3 ft) high stems; spread 30 cm (12 in).

Cautleya

This is an unusual, exotic-looking plant with long, broad leaves and, in summer, spikes of yellow flowers. It looks rather like a tropical canna. Needs moist soil. Height 1.2 m (4 ft), spread 60 cm (2 ft).

Cynoglossum (hound's tongue)

Herbaceous plants best grown in fertile soil with good drainage. Beautiful blue, myosotis-like flowers are carried in early to mid-summer by *C. nervosum*. Height up to 60 cm (2 ft), spread 30 cm (12 in).

Shrubs need not be dismal because they grow in the shade. *Vibernum opulus compactum*, for example, bears heavy clusters of rich scarlet fruits. Hostas are happy in a similar position.

Dicentra

Herbaceous plants with attractive ferny foliage and hanging heart-shaped flowers. Ideal for the mixed border is *D. spectabilis* (bleeding heart), with pinkish-red and white blooms in late spring/early summer. Height up to 60 cm (2 ft), spread 45 cm (18 in). Plant in a sheltered position with humus-rich soil and leave undisturbed.

Epimedium (barrenwort)

Attractive ground-cover plants, ideal for dry shade, with attractive foliage, often flushed bronze in spring and taking on tints in the autumn. Height and spread up to 30 cm (12 in). There are many species, producing dainty sprays of flowers in spring or early summer, like *E. macranthum* 'Rose Queen', deep pink; *E. rubrum*, red; *E. sulphureum*, pale yellow; *E. warleyense*, orange; and *E. youngianum* 'Niveum', white.

Euphorbia (spurge)

Many of the herbaceous and sub-shrubby species are bold, distinctive plants for shade. The tiny flowers are surrounded by showy petal-like bracts. One of the most dramatic species is *E. wulfenii*, a sub-shrub with a height and spread of 1.2 m (4 ft). The glaucous leaves are evergreen and in spring and summer the plant sports large greeny yellow flower heads. Equally impressive is *E. characias*, of herbaceous habit, height and spread up to 1.2 m (4 ft), with greyish foliage and large acid-yellow flower heads in spring/early summer. The herbaceous *E. griffthii* 'Fireglow' has brilliant red-orange flower heads in spring/early summer; height and spread 60 cm (2 ft). The low bushy sub-shrub, *E. epithymoides*, is covered with acid yellow flowers in spring; height and spread 45 cm (18 in).

Geranium (crane's-bill)

Several of these herbaceous perennials thrive in shade, including the varieties of *G. endressii*. Height and spread approximately 45 cm (18 in); flowering season late spring to late summer. Well-known varieties include 'A.T. Johnson', light pink; and 'Wargrave Pink', pure pink.

Helleborus

This genus contains some distinctive herbaceous and evergreen species. Best grown in moist soil with plenty of humus. Do not disturb after planting. Well-known is *H. orientalis* (Lenten rose), with saucer-shaped flowers in late winter/early spring. Comes in a range of colours, including shades of pink, purple, red, cream and white. Evergreen foliage; height and spread about 45 cm (18 in). Don't be put off by the common name of *H. foetidus* (stinking hellebore), as it is a fine plant for shade, producing clusters of yellowish-green flowers in spring above attractive evergreen foliage. Height and spread 60 cm (2 ft). Less often seen in gardens is *H. atrorubens* with very dark purple flowers in winter and spring. Height 30 cm (12 in), spread 45 cm (18 in). Another species all too rarely seen is *H. purpurascens*, also with purple flowers, produced during spring. Height and spread approximately 30 cm (12 in). *H. argutifolius* is a distinctive plant with boldly lobed evergreen leaves and clustered heads of greenish-yellow flowers in spring. Height and spread 60 cm (2 ft). Finally, we must not forget *H. niger* (Christmas rose), whose large flattish white flowers are produced between early winter and early spring. A good variety is 'Potter's Wheel' with extra-large blooms. The Christmas rose is evergreen and has a height and spread of 30 cm (12 in).

Hemerocallis (day lily)
Herbaceous plants forming bold clumps of grassy foliage and lily-like flowers in summer/autumn. Each flower lasts for only one day, but blooms are produced in succession. Height and spread 60–90 cm (2–3 ft). Best in moist soil; leave undisturbed once planted. There are many hybrids to choose from and here is a small selection: 'Black Magic', reddish mahogany; 'Doubloon', deep yellow; 'Pink Damask', pink; and 'Stafford', deep red. New American varieties are now available in the UK, including 'Anzac', brilliant red; 'Cherry Cheeks', cherry red; and 'Luxury Lace', pink with green throat.

Hosta (plantain lily)
The hostas are grown primarily for their large bold deciduous leaves which come in all shades of green and many variegations. They flower from mid-summer to early autumn, producing spikes of lily-like flowers in shades of mauve, lilac or white. Heights vary according to species or variety: from 30 to 90 cm (1–3 ft). Planting distance varies according to vigour, but ranges from 45–60 cm (18–24 in). Here's a small selection from which to choose:
Green-leaved hostas: 'Big Daddy', blue-green; *H. fortunei*, greyish green; 'Honeybells'; and *H. sieboldiana* 'Elegans', blue-green.
Golden hostas: *H. fortunei* 'Aurea'; 'Gold Edger'; 'Gold Standard'; 'Golden Medallion'; 'Golden Prayers'; 'Piedmont Gold'; and 'Sun Power'.
Variegated hostas: *H. crispula; H. fortunei* 'Aureomarginata'; 'Frances Williams'; 'Ginkgo Craig'; 'Thomas Hogg'; *H. undulata* 'Medio-variegata'; and *H. ventricosa* 'Variegata'.
   Hostas should be planted in moisture-retentive humus-rich soil. Guard against slugs.

Phlox

The border phlox, varieties of *P. paniculata*, generally grow and flower better in light shade. The white varieties show up well, of course, in shady borders. Soil should be moisture-retentive for optimum growth. There are many varieties in shades of red, pink, orange, blue, etc. Flowering period is mid-summer to early autumn. Average height 90 cm (3 ft), spread 45 cm (18 in).

Polygonum (knotweed)

Many of the knotweeds will grow in shade but some are rather invasive. Not so *P. bistorta* 'Superbum', of herbaceous habit with bold spikes of pure pink flowers in late spring and early summer. Height 90 cm (3 ft), spread 60 cm (2 ft).

Pulmonaria (lungwort)

These are attractive, small, spring-flowering herbaceous plants suitable for dry or moist shade. *P. angustifolia* has beautiful blue flowers: height and spread 30 cm (12 in). Varieties of *P. saccharata* include 'Sissinghurst White', white flowers; *P. s. argentea*, blue flowers, silvery foliage; and 'Bowles Red', red flowers. Height and spread 30 cm (12 in).

Tellima

The evergreen perennial *T. grandiflora* is suitable for growing in dry shade and its foliage makes effective ground cover. The lobed leaves are fresh green and in spring and summer spikes of tiny yellowish green flowers are produced. Height and spread 45 cm (18 in).

Tradescantia (spiderwort)

The herbaceous *T. × andersoniana* varieties have grassy foliage and a long succession of three-petalled flowers from early summer to early autumn. Best grown in moist soil. Varieties come mainly in shades of blue or purple, also white. 'Isis', deep blue; 'Osprey', white; 'Purple Dome', purple; 'Zwanenburg Blue', pure blue.

Viola (violet)

There are many violas which thrive in moist shade but one of my favourites is *V. cornuta* with large blue flowers in summer. There is also a white variety, 'Alba'. Height and spread up to 30 cm (12 in).

BULBS
Colchicum (autumn crocus)

The autumn-flowering colchicums are excellent for planting around large shrubs, where their long leaves, which appear in the spring, will not be a nuisance. The flowers are rather like those of crocuses. Plant in late summer, 10 cm (4 in) deep. Species include *C. autumnale*, mauve-pink flowers, flowering height 15 cm (6 in), plant 20 cm (8 in) apart; and *C. speciosum* with mauve blooms, flowering height 15 cm (6 in), plant 30 cm (12 in) apart. There are several hybrids available, too, like 'Autumn Queen', bluish-purple; 'Lilac Wonder', dark lilac; 'The Giant', mauve; and 'Waterlily', double mauve blooms. Height and planting distance as for *C. speciosum*, which is one of the parents of these hybrids.

Fritillaria

An aristocratic bulb for the mixed border is *F. imperialis* (crown imperial), with clusters of bell-shaped flowers on 60–90 cm (2–3 ft) high stems in spring. The colour may be orange, red or yellow. Plant in early autumn, 30 cm (12 in) apart and 20 cm (8 in) deep. Do not disturb once planted. Soil should be well-drained.

Galanthus (snowdrop)

Every border should have drifts of winter-flowering snowdrops around shrubs and other plants. The common snowdrop, *G. nivalis*, is the best-known with pendulous, white, green-marked flowers. Height 8–20 cm (3–8 in). There are numerous varieties, like the double-flowered 'Floreplena', and the larger-flowered and taller 'S. Arnott'. *G. elwesii* is a desirable species with broad foliage and white and dark green flowers. Height 15–20 cm (6–8 in). Best grown in moist soil. Ideally plant bulbs immediately after flowering, while in leaf; otherwise dormant bulbs in autumn. Plant about 8 cm (3 in) deep and 8–10 cm (3–4 in) apart.

Galtonia (summer hyacinth)

G. candicans makes a marvellous companion for shrubs with its strap-shaped leaves and late-summer spikes of pendulous, white, bell-shaped flowers. Height 1.2 m (4 ft). Plant 20 cm (8 in) apart and 15–20 cm (6–8 in) deep in spring.

Muscari (grape hyacinth)

Well-known, small spring-flowering bulbs with short fat spikes of mainly blue flowers, ideal for drifting among shrubs and other plants. There are several species including *M. armeniacum* with dark blue flowers, height 20 cm (8 in); *M. botryoides*, also dark blue, similar height; and *M. tubergenianum* (syn. *M. aucheri*), with spikes of deep and light blue flowers, height 20 cm (8 in). Plant bulbs 8 cm (3 in) deep in autumn, spacing them 8 cm (3 in) apart.

Narcissus (daffodil)

Undoubtedly the most popular spring-flowering bulbs, thriving in fertile moist soil. There are many species and hundreds of hybrids to choose from. For the mixed border the large trumpet daffodils take some beating, like the well-known 'Golden Harvest' and the white 'Mount Hood'. (White daffodils show up especially well in shade). Or you may prefer the smaller *cyclamineus* hybrids with long trumpet and swept-back petals, like 'February Gold', 'Peeping Tom' (yellow), or 'Jack Snipe', cream and yellow. Plant daffodils in late summer/early autumn, about 15 cm (6 in) deep and 15–20 cm (6–8 in) apart.

Ornithogalum (star of Bethlehem)

Easy-going bulbs which look lovely drifted around dark green shrubs, where their white flowers show up well. *O. nutans* blooms in spring; it has bell-shaped flowers on stems up to 45 cm (18 in) in height. *O. umbellatum* flowers at the same time and has masses of starry blooms. Height 30 cm (12 in). Plant the bulbs in autumn, about 8 cm (3 in) deep and 15 cm (6 in) apart.

Scilla (squill)

There are few more charming sights in spring than carpets of blue squills drifting among spring-flowering shrubs. Of the several species available *S. sibirica* is particularly recommended with its vivid blue bell-shaped flowers in profusion. Height 15 cm (6 in). Similar is *S. tubergeniana* but the striped blooms are lighter blue. Height 10 cm (4 in). Plant scillas during autumn in moisture-retentive soil, 8 cm (3 in) deep and 8–10 cm (3–4 in) apart.

CHAPTER 4

SHADY WALLS

One should make the most of vertical space in a garden by growing climbing plants on walls and fences. Although many like warm sunny walls, there is no shortage of climbers for those which are in shade, as with a north-facing wall, provided the light is bright.

Also, if you have a dark gloomy corner (for example, created by buildings) why not consider brightening it up by planting some gold- and silver-variegated shrubs and other plants? Many people erroneously think that these will not succeed in shade; but in fact there is a surprisingly large number that will thrive in these conditions.

As with borders, do try to create some attractive planting schemes with climbers and wall shrubs. For example, a particularly lovely combination for winter is *Garrya elliptica*, which has evergreen foliage

Fig. 7 An attractive combination of wall shrubs for winter colour. On the right is the evergreen *Garrya elliptica*, which bears greyish catkins, and nestling up to this is *Jasminum nudiflorum* (winter jasmine) with bright yellow flowers.

and greyish catkins, with the yellow flowers of *Jasminum nudiflorum* (winter jasmine) (Fig. 7).

A classic arrangement is to have clematis or white *Jasminum officinale* intertwining with climbing roses (yes, there are some roses which will flower on a north-facing wall).

Another combination which really comes into its own in autumn is *Parthenocissus quinquefolia* (Virginia creeper), with its fiery autumn tints, and *Hedera canariensis* 'Variegata' (variegated Canary Island ivy) with contrasting white and green variegated foliage.

Do try these, and other combinations of your choice, as plants look so much better when they have suitable 'neighbours'.

CLIMBERS AND WALL SHRUBS

Berberidopsis
The evergreen shrub *B. corallina* is best grown in acid to neutral, moist, humus-rich soil. It is not completely hardy and best avoided in areas prone to hard winters. Pendulous crimson flowers are produced in summer and show up well against the dark spine-edged leaves. Height and spread 1.8 m (6 ft) or more.

Chaenomeles (ornamental quince)
These deciduous shrubs have apple-blossom-like flowers during spring in shades of red, orange, pink and also white, followed by aromatic fruits. The white varieties show up well on a shady wall. Varieties of *C. speciosa* are widely grown. Height and spread at least 1.8 m (6 ft). If the weather is mild blooms may start to appear in mid-winter. The best white variety is 'Nivalis'. Also showing up well on a shady wall is 'Apple Blossom', whose white blooms are tinted with pink. A good pink variety is 'Phylis Moore' with double flowers, while if a stronger colour is desired, 'Crimson and Gold' takes some beating, with gold stamens and red petals.

Clematis
A number of clematis will flourish on a north-facing wall and look lovely in association with other plants like roses, chaenomeles (choose early-flowering clematis), lonicera and pyracantha. Try the following species: *C. alpina*, blue flowers in spring, height and spread about 1.8 m (6 ft); *C. macropetala*, flowers in pale and deep blue, produced in spring and early summer, height 3.6 m (12 ft), spread 1.8 m (6 ft); *C. montana*, a vigorous species with white flowers in spring, or pink in varieties 'Elizabeth' and 'Rubens', height 12 m (40 ft), spread 18 m (20 ft); *C. orientalis*, fragrant yellow flowers in late summer/autumn, height 18 m (20 ft),

A pleasant gold and silver mixture can be contrived in dappled, though not deep shade. Here are *Ribes* 'Brocklebanki', *Lamium maculatum* 'Aureum' and *Carex riparia* 'Aurea' with *Lamium* 'Beacon Silver'.

spread 3 m (10 ft); and *C. tangutica*, rather like *C. orientalis*. Some of the large-flowered hybrids are suitable for north-facing walls: how about trying the popular 'Nellie Moser' with pink, crimson-striped flowers in summer, height about 3 m (10 ft), spread about 1.8 m (6 ft). Clematis thrive in chalky soils.

Cotoneaster
The fishbone cotoneaster, *C. horizontalis*, is a deciduous shrub which is amenable to training flat, when it will grow to approximately 2.4 m (8 ft) in height and spread. It has tiny rounded leaves, colouring well in autumn, and masses of red berries which last well into winter if the birds leave them alone. The form *C. h.* 'Variegatus' has very distinctive white variegated foliage, which shows up well. It is a slower grower than the species.

Garrya
The evergreen shrub *G. elliptica* bears greyish-green catkins during winter. These are most showy on male plants (females having smaller catkins). A good variety is 'James Roof' with ultra-long catkins. Height up to 4.5 m (15 ft), spread up to 3.6 m (12 ft). An excellent companion for *Jasminum nudiflorum*.

Hedera
The ornamental ivies are excellent for shady walls and look good with various other plants such as parthenocissus, berberidopsis and cotoneaster. Of the large-leaved ivies I can recommend *H. canariensis* 'Variegata' (variegated Canary Island ivy) with deep green and white variegated leaves; and *H. colchica* 'Dentata Variegata' with light green and cream variegation. Height of both about 6 m (20 ft), spread approximately 3–4.5 m (10–15 ft). *H. helix* is a small-leaved ivy, capable of reaching a height of at least 15 m (50 ft). The species is not usually grown, but rather the many attractive varieties like 'Buttercup', deep yellow leaves; 'Glacier', silvery-grey and white; 'Gold Child', yellow-edged leaves; and 'Goldheart', foliage splashed with yellow. To prevent ivies becoming too heavy, prune them hard back to the wall each year in early spring.

Hydrangea
The climbing hydrangea, *H. petiolaris*, is a deciduous climber capable of reaching a height of at least 7.5 m (25 ft), with a spread of at least 3 m (10 ft). It has white flowers, carried in flat heads, during summer. Best grown in moist soil. Supports itself by means of aerial roots (roots produced on the stems).

Jasminum (jasmine)

J. nudiflorum (winter jasmine) is a deciduous climber with bright yellow blooms in winter. It will reach a height of about 3 m (10 ft) with a spread of about 1.8 m (6 ft). After flowering, prune back old flowered shoots to within 5 cm (2 in) of their base. *J. officinale* (summer jasmine) produces white, scented flowers from early summer to mid-autumn. Height up to 9 m (30 ft), spread at least half of this.

Kerria (Jew's mallow)

The deciduous shrub *K. japonica* 'Pleniflora' is recommended for growing against a shady wall when, in spring, it sports double yellowish-orange flowers in profusion. Height up to 3.6 m (12 ft), spread up to 1.8 m (6 ft). Prune after flowering by cutting out completely all the old shoots which flowered. New shoots arise from the base.

Lonicera (honeysuckle)

Several honeysuckles will flourish on a shady wall. *L. caprifolium* (perfoliate woodbine) is a strong-growing deciduous species which climbs to a height of 6 m (20 ft), with a spread of at least 3 m (10 ft). The fragrant creamy flowers, flushed pink, are produced in summer. *L. japonica* 'Halliana' bears highly fragrant white blooms in summer; and *L. j.* 'Aureoreticulata' has conspicuous yellow-veined leaves. Both are evergreen or semi-evergreen and can reach a height of at least 7.5 m (25 ft), with a spread of about half this. L. × *tellmanniana* is a deciduous species with yellow and red blooms in summer. Height 4.5 m (15 ft), spread 2.4 m (8 ft). Honeysuckles like a humus-rich soil.

Parthenocissus (Virginia creeper)

The Virginia creepers are self-supporting climbers noted for brilliant autumn leaf colour. Most are very vigorous but can be contained by cutting them back in summer. The best-known species is *P. quinquefolia* which is capable of reaching a height of at least 18 m (60 ft). It will spread to cover a very large area if desired. The leaves turn bright red in the autumn. *P. henryana* (Chinese Virginia creeper) grows to about half the height of *P. quinquefolia* and will also spread over a wide area. It has deep green foliage variegated with pink and white. In autumn it takes on bright red tints.

Pyracantha (firethorn)

Evergreen shrubs which can be trained flat against a wall and bearing heavy crops of red, orange or yellow berries in autumn and winter. There are several popular species like *P. angustifolia*, height 3 m (10 ft), spread 2.4 m (8 ft), orange berries; *P. atalantioides*, height and spread about 3.6 m (12 ft), red berries, or yellow in variety 'Aurea'; *P. coccinea* 'Lalandei', height and spread about 3.6 m (12 ft), reddish-orange berries; and *P. crenulata*, height about 3 m (10 ft), spread at least 3.6 m (12 ft), reddish-orange berries in variety *P. c. rogersiana*, yellow in 'Flava', and orange in 'Orange Glow' and 'Mohave'.

Rosa (rose)

Several climbing roses are suitable for north-facing walls. Of the modern repeat-flowering climbers I can recommend 'Aloha', pink, height 2.4 m (8 ft); 'Danse du Feu', orange-red, height 3 m (10 ft); 'Dortmund', red, white centre, height 3.6 m (12 ft); 'Golden Showers', yellow, height 2.4 m (8 ft); 'Maigold', yellow, height 3 m (10 ft); 'New Dawn', pale pink, height 1.8 m (6 ft); and 'Sympathie', scarlet, height 3 m (10 ft). Old climbers include 'Mermaid', large pale yellow, height about 6 m (20 ft); and 'Mme Alfred Carrière', white, tinted pink, height about 3.6 m (10 ft). Provide a moisture-retentive fertile soil. Prune in early spring by cutting back side shoots to leave one to three growth buds.

Schizophragma

A self-clinging deciduous climber, *S. hydrangeoides* has attractive dark green foliage and, in summer, big flat heads of cream flowers. Height up to 9 m (30 ft), spread about half of this. Needs a moist, humus-rich fertile soil. Cut off dead flower heads.

PLANTS FOR GLOOMY CORNERS

Dark gloomy corners can be brightened up by planting gold- and silver-variegated shrubs and other plants. Choose those that succeed in shade.

Aucuba (spotted laurel)

Evergreen shrubs which were a feature of sombre Victorian 'shrubberies'. However, varieties with gold variegated or mottled leaves are very bright and won't create a sombre atmosphere, especially if combined with more 'airy' subjects such as *Cornus alba* 'Elegantissima' and *Phalaris arundinacea* 'Picta' (see below). There are several good varieties of *Aucuba japonica*, height and spread in excess of 1.8 m (6 ft), including 'Crotonifolia', speckled gold; 'Gold Dust', similar; 'Picturata', splashed with gold; and 'Variegata', blotched with yellow.

Cornus (dogwood)

Some varieties of *C. alba* have attractive variegated foliage, including

Unlike most of the hydrangeas one sees, *H. petiolaris* is a strong-growing climber which bears many clusters of white 'lace-cap' flowers once well established.

Japanese flowering quinces, *Chaenomeles speciosa*, once known as 'japonicas', smother themselves in blossom in early spring before their leaves appear. This is 'Moerloosii'.

'Elegantissima', white and green; 'Spaethii', gold-edged; and 'Variegata', cream-edged. 'Aurea' has yellow foliage. These shrubs are deciduous and have red stems. Height and spread 2.4 m (8 ft). Best in moist soil. Each year, in early spring, cut stems down to within a few centimetres of the ground.

Elaeagnus
Evergreen shrubs with gold-variegated foliage. Varieties of *E. pungens* are best-known, height and spread 2.4–6 m (8–12 ft). Fairly slow growing. I

can recommend 'Maculata', irregularly splashed with gold; and 'Dicksonii', yellow-edged leaves. *E.* × *ebbingei*, of similar stature, has some attractive varieties, too, especially 'Gilt Edge', foliage edged deep yellow; and 'Limelight', leaves blotched gold in the centre. Prune out any shoots with plain green leaves.

Euonymus (spindle)
Some of the evergreen shrubs can be recommended, like varieties of *E. fortunei*. Try 'Emerald and Gold' with yellow and green leaves, and 'Silver Queen' whose foliage is edged with white. Both are low spreading shrubs. *E. japonicus* varieties can be recommended, too; height at least 3 m (10 ft), spread about 1.8 m (6 ft). Try 'Aureopictus' with gold-centred leaves; 'Macrophyllus Albus', white-edged leaves; and 'Ovatus Aureus', cream-edged leaves.

Ilex (holly)
Variegated hollies are ideal evergreen shrubs for shade. They are slow growing. *I.* × *altaclarensis*, height up to 9 m (30 ft), spread about 4.5 m (15 ft), has some good varieties like 'Golden King', gold-edged, almost spineless leaves; and 'Lawsoniana', leaves splashed yellow in centre, usually spineless. There are many variegated varieties of *I. aquifolium* (common holly), height up to 7 m (25 ft), spread 3.6 m (12 ft), like 'Argentea Marginata', white-edged leaves; 'Golden Queen', yellow-edged leaves; 'Handsworth New Silver', mottled grey, white margin; 'Silver Milkboy', blotched cream in centre; and 'Silver Queen', cream-edged leaves.

Lamium (dead nettle)
The hardy perennial *L. maculatum* 'Aureum' has beautiful deep yellow foliage. It is a slow-growing plant, with a height and spread of about 20 cm (8 in), and needs a moisture-retentive, fertile soil.

Ligustrum (privet)
L. ovalifolium 'Aureum' is the ubiquitous golden privet which makes a very bright display with its rich yellow leaves, which are usually evergreen, but may be deciduous in very severe winter weather. Height and spread up to about 3 m (10 ft). *L. lucidum* 'Tricolor' is a small evergreen tree with white-edged leaves which are tinted pink when they unfurl. Height at least 6 m (20 ft) with a spread of about half this.

Milium (millet)
A beautiful little grass for shade is *M. effusum* 'Aureum' (golden wood

millet), with bright golden arching foliage up to 30 cm (12 in) long. It is a clump-forming perennial, best grown in shade, and needs a moisure-retentive soil.

Phalaris

The ornamental grass, *P. arundinacea* 'Picta' (gardener's garters), is a most attractive plant, if rather invasive. Plant it where it will not swamp other plants. The foliage is striped with white and green, giving a very light, airy effect in a gloomy corner. Height 60 cm (2 ft). Plant 60 cm (2 ft) apart.

Philadelphus (mock orange)

The golden mock orange, *P. coronarius* 'Aureus', is a deciduous shrub with brilliant yellow foliage. Eventually it becomes greener. In early summer heavily scented white blossoms are produced. Height and spread 1.8–2.4 m (6–8 ft). Oldest shoots can be thinned out as soon as flowering has finished.

Santolina (cotton lavender)

The dwarf evergreen shrub *S. neapolitana* forms a dense rounded bush with aromatic feathery grey foliage. Yellow flowers in summer, although these may not be freely produced in shade. Height and spread about 60 cm (2 ft). If plants become straggly after a few years, cut them hard back in mid-spring.

CHAPTER 5

STEEP BANKS

A 'gardening problem' worrying many people is how to deal with a steep bank. Access is difficult, and the soil may be loose and inclined to be washed down during heavy rain. If the bank is in shade it seems there is no hope of doing anything with it.

Those faced with such a situation should take heart from the fact that they have an asset rather than a problem. For a start, an undulating garden is more interesting than a perfectly flat plot. It is comparatively easy to get over the problem of access; and there is no shortage of shade-loving plants that can be used to densely clothe the bank, to create a 'tapestry' of flower and foliage colour and stabilize the soil.

I would forget about grassing the bank (a common practice) because not only is it difficult to cut, it is also the least attractive method of covering a bank. Besides, you will probably already have a lawn in another part of the garden.

Terracing a bank can be a most attractive way of retaining the soil, creating a series of level areas for planting. But this idea has a major drawback – it can be prohibitively expensive, particularly if brick or stone retaining walls are used.

What I have done with my own steep bank is plant it densely with low growing, shade loving ground-cover plants. These create a pleasing texture and as they close up together and their roots ramify the soil, the bank is stabilized. No amount of rain can wash the soil away.

I would not advise disturbing the soil too much before planting as this can loosen it even more (see Page 22), but it is sensible to try to make access easier. You need some level footholds, from which you can work and carry out any plant maintenance, such as weeding in the early stages. Remember that once plants are established and have completely covered the bank there will be little need for access.

Excellent footholds can be created by sinking sections of tree trunks, 15–30 cm (6–12 in) thick, into the bank, making sure the tops are perfectly level. These could be arranged like stepping stones if desired, or in the form of steps, setting one above the other (Fig. 8). On my bank I created steps with tree-trunk sections, and very good they look too. The life of the timber can be considerably extended by treating the sections

Fig. 8 Sections of tree trunk can be used to form steps in a steep bank. On either side of these steps are drifts of variegated ivy (left) and *Ruscus aculeatus* (butcher's broom) (right), both excellent ground-cover plants for dry banks.

with a horticultural wood preservative before they are set in place. You should first remove the bark.

If you cannot obtain tree-trunk sections then consider using flat pieces of natural stone in the same way.

WAYS OF CREATING A 'TAPESTRY'

Presuming you intend using a number of different ground-cover plants, rather than a single subject, bear in mind there are various ways of arranging them. You could create a patchwork effect – bold, irregular groups of each subject.

A more unusual way of arranging plants is to have 'drifts' of each subject meandering down the bank, rather like a stream of cascade of water. In other words, wide, winding 'ribbons' of plants (Fig. 9). Different subjects could be arranged so that they contrast with each other in colour and texture. Ideas for combinations of plants are given later in this chapter, when plants suited to shady banks are described.

It is important to space the plants correctly so that they quickly close up and completely cover the soil. Optimum planting distances have been given with the plant descriptions.

I would stress the importance of having sufficiently large groups or drifts of each subject, even if you have only a small bank. Lots of very

Fig. 9 Drifts of ground-cover plants meandering down a steep bank. On the left is *Juniperus sabina tamariscifolia* (juniper) with feathery grey-blue foliage, and on the right *Mahonia aquifolium* (Oregon grape) with yellow flowers in spring. Both are suitable for ordinary to moist soils.

tiny patches create a fussy, 'spotty' effect. With limited space it is better to opt for fewer subjects and to plant them boldly.

PLANTS FOR DRY SOIL

The soil forming a bank can be very well drained, so much so that for much of the time the soil is on the dry side. This, coupled with shade, limits the range of plants that can be grown. Nevertheless, some attractive schemes can be created in these conditions.

A very tolerant evergreen shrubby ground-cover plant is *Ruscus aculeatus* (butcher's broom). It does not produce leaves but has flattened stems which look like leaves. These are deep green and spiny. Male and female flowers are carried on separate plants and in the autumn the females produce large red berries. It is necessary to plant ruscus in reasonably large groups to ensure you have both male and female plants, so that berries are produced. Height ranges from 60–90 cm (2–3 ft); plant 60 cm apart.

A large planting of ruscus can look rather sombre unless combined with a lighter-coloured plant. What about *Galeobdolon luteum* 'Variegatum' (syn. *Lamiastrum galeobdolon* 'Variegatum', *Lamium galeobdolon* 'Variegatum') (yellow archangel)? This evergreen perennial has beautiful silver-splashed foliage and it spreads by long trailing stems, which root into the soil. In early summer spikes of yellow blooms are produced. Let it partially intermingle with the ruscus, but bear in mind that galeobdolon is an extremely vigorous plant and needs space to develop. However, if it outgrows its allotted space it is easily dug out with a fork. Height 15–30 cm (6–12 in). Plant 45–60 cm (18–24 in) apart.

The variegated hederas (ivies) also make excellent companions for ruscus and, like the latter, are also evergreen. I have described a good selection on Page 43. Although ivies are thought of as climbing plants they do in fact make excellent ground cover. And they are adaptable as regards soil, being equally at home in dry conditions or moist soil. They will form a carpet up to 30 cm (12 in) in height. Large-leaved ivies can be planted about 90 cm (3 ft) apart, and the small-leaved kinds 60–90 cm (2–3 ft) apart.

You may wish to include some plain green ivies on your bank, some of which create a marvellous texture when mass planted. Choose varieties of *Hedera helix*, like 'Bird's Foot', 'Caenwoodiana', 'Digitata', 'Green Ripple', 'Sagittifolia' and 'Shamrock'. These all have conspicuously lobed leaves.

It is best to buy ivies specially grown for ground cover rather than those intended for use as climbers, as it is difficult to get the latter to lie flat when planting.

The ubiquitous *Hypericum calycinum* (St John's wort) should not be despised for ground cover in dry shady conditions. Although not very interesting when out of flower, it is nevertheless an excellent plant for stabilizing banks, ramifying the soil with stolons or underground stems. It also makes an excellent display throughout summer, with large deep yellow flowers which have conspicuous stamens. The foliage is evergreen. Height 30–45 cm (12–18 in). Plant 45 cm (18 in) apart. Cut the stems down almost to ground level each year in mid-spring to ensure really dense ground cover. To provide interest in the winter you could plant variegated ivies next to hypericum.

Another good companion for the hypericum is early to mid-summer flowering *Geranium macrorrhizum* (crane's bill), with pink flowers and highly aromatic foliage (noticeable only when bruised). There is also a white form called 'Album'. Height about 30 cm (12 in); plant 45 cm (18 in) apart.

PLANTS FOR ORDINARY TO MOIST SOIL
If the soil is not prone to excessive drying out, or indeed is moisture-retentive, then you have a choice of a much wider range of ground-cover plants.

There are several plants, for instance, for acid or lime-free soils.

Gaultheria procumbens (partridge berry) is recommended, a prostrate creeping evergreen shrub no more than 15 cm (6 in) in height. The small white or pink urn-shaped flowers appear in summer and are followed by conspicuous red berries. Not recommended under trees, as it hates drips from branches. Plant 30–38 cm (12–15 in) apart.

Next to the gaultheria, and contrasting well with it, I suggest one of the ground-cover polygonums (knotweed) with poker-like spikes of pink or red flowers in late summer and autumn. These grow in acid or

Hypericum calycinum, or rose of Sharon, makes strong-growing ground cover under trees, with the bonus of bold golden flowers where there is sufficient sun.

alkaline soils. *P. affine* has deep pink flowers, grows to about 15 cm (6 in) in height and should be planted 45 cm (18 in) apart. *P. vacciniifolium* is evergreen and has pinky-red flowers. Height 15 cm (6 in); planting distance 45 cm (18 in).

An evergreen berrying shrub which must have moist acid soil is *Pernettya mucronata*. It has small deep green shiny foliage, small white flowers in early summer and large marble-like berries in the autumn, in shades of pink, red, purple and white. It is essential to grow both male and female plants for berries to be produced. There are numerous varieties to choose from. In time, the plants may become too tall and straggly, in which case they can be pruned back hard in early spring. Height may be up to 1.5 m (5 ft). Plant 60 cm (2 ft) apart.

Vaccinium vitis-idaea (mountain cranberry, cowberry) needs the same conditions as pernettya. A carpeting evergreen shrub, it has shiny deep green foliage, white urn-shaped blooms in early summer and edible deep red berries in autumn and winter. Height about 15 cm (6 in); plant 30 cm (12 in) apart. Trim the plants in mid-spring to maintain dense growth.

Several juniperus species (junipers) will take quite deep shade and make good dense evergreen ground cover, like *J.* × *media* 'Pfitzerana' which forms layers of feathery, slightly prickly green foliage. Height about 90 cm (3 ft); planting distance 1.2 m (4 ft). *J. sabina tamariscifolia* forms really dense cover with its layers of horizontal branches and feathery grey-blue foliage. Height up to 45 cm (18 in); planting distance 60 cm (2 ft).

An evergreen shrub which contrasts well in shape and texture with these junipers is *Mahonia aquifolium* (Oregon grape). This shrub spreads by suckers and certainly helps to stabilize loose soil. The handsome shiny deep green foliage makes an excellent background for the heads of yellow, scented blooms which are produced in spring and followed by clusters of black berries. Height 90–120 cm (3–4 ft); planting distance 60 cm (2 ft). To ensure a really dense habit cut the stems back hard each year in mid-spring. This, of course, will result in loss of berries.

The dwarf viburnum, *V. davidii*, is an aristocratic evergreen shrub with very handsome foliage. The large oval leaves are deep green with conspicuous veins; white flowers are borne in early summer and followed by striking blue-green berries if plants of each sex are grouped together. Height approximately 60 cm (2 ft); plant about 60 cm (2 ft) apart.

How about creating some blue 'streams' with dwarf flowering plants? Ideal for this purpose are two campanulas (bellflowers), although they are very vigorous and perhaps not the best choice for very small banks. *C. portenschlagiana* has a dense mass of medium-green rounded leaves and throughout summer is covered with bell-shaped, fairly deep blue flowers. Height 15 cm (6 in); planting distance 45 cm (18 in). *C. poschars-kyana* is even more vigorous than the above species, carries similar foliage, and throughout summer bears a profusion of blue starry flowers. Height 30 cm (12 in); planting distance 60 cm (2 ft).

A more restrained blue 'stream' could be created with *Vinca minor* (lesser periwinkle), which has starry blue flowers during spring and into summer, set against mats of shiny deep green evergreen foliage. There are several varieties with blue flowers, like the double 'Azurea Flore Pleno', and 'Bowles' Variety'. Height 5–10 cm (2–4 in); planting distance 45 cm (18 in).

A stream of vincas would look good trickling through groups of hydrangeas. These are not strictly ground-cover plants but are often used on banks where the soil is moisture-retentive. I have planted part of my bank with hydrangeas, in the dappled shade of trees, and they are a marvellous sight in summer and autumn. Furthermore, hydrangeas are excellent value for money and one can fill quite a large area relatively inexpensively.

I recommend the hortensia and lacecap groups of *Hydrangea macro-phylla*. The hortensias have huge mop-like heads of flowers, at least 15 cm (6 in) in diameter. The lacecaps have flat heads of a similar diameter, which look rather like lace tablemats! Varieties are mainly blue or pink but the colour will depend on the soil: in acid soils pink hydrangeas will be blue while on alkaline soils blue varieties will be pink. There are also white varieties, which are unaffected by soil type.

These hydrangeas are deciduous and form rounded bushes to a height of 1.2–1.8 m (4–6 ft). This is also the recommended planting distance.

There are lots of varieties in both groups. Of the hortensias, I can recommend 'Altona', bright pink or blue; 'Deutschland', dark pink or blue; Générale Vicomtesse de Vibraye', bright pink or blue; 'Hamburg', dark pink or blue; 'Madame E. Mouillière', white, only recommended for mild areas; and 'Marechal Foch', rose-pink, or purple/dark blue.

My favourite lacecaps include 'Blue Wave', pink or blue flowers; 'Lanarth White', bright pink or blue, edged with white; 'Mariesii', rose-pink or deep blue; 'Sea Foam', blue and white flowers; and 'White Wave', white.

Hydrangeas grow best in a position sheltered from cold winds and where early morning sun cannot damage frozen flower buds and new growth. Carefully cut off dead flower heads in early spring, making sure you do not damage the buds below. Stems which are at least three years old can be cut out completely at this time to make way for new growth.

Another plant which associates well with hydrangeas when drifted around them is evergreen × *Fatshedera lizei*. It is a hybrid of *Fatsia japonica* 'Moseri' and *Hedera helix hibernica* (Irish ivy), with large lobed dark green glossy leaves. When grown as ground cover allow one plant per sq m (sq yd).

Ajugas are excellent carpeting ground-cover plants for shady banks provided the soil is moisture-retentive. Varieties of *A. reptans* (bugle) are especially recommended, with a height, when in flower, of 15–30 cm (6–12 in) and a spread of 30–45 cm (12–18 in). Flowering period is early to mid-summer, the blooms being carried in spikes. The usual colour is blue. A fairly recent introduction is 'Braunherz', with purplish-bronze foliage and dark blue flowers. Well-known is 'Burgundy Glow' with multicoloured foliage, but predominantly wine-red. Flowers are light blue. 'Purpurea' and 'Variegata' are widely planted, the former having red-purple foliage and the latter variegated pale green and cream.

CHAPTER 6

CONTAINERS AND SEASONAL BEDS

Shade-tolerant plants for patio beds and containers seems a contradiction in terms, for we think of patios as being sunny areas. However, I must cater for all needs and for those gardeners whose patios are in shade for all or part of the day I offer a wide range of colourful plants and bulbs for their tubs, window boxes, hanging baskets and indeed small patio beds. The courtyard – an area which is invariably in shade due to the surrounding walls – is also often furnished with containers of plants. Here again we must use shade-tolerant kinds if worthwhile displays are to be achieved.

The most popular plants for ornamental containers and patio beds are undoubtedly spring and summer bedding plants, annuals and bulbs, because they give such a good and long show of colour. So here I will consider shade-tolerant subjects from these groups.

Fig. 10 A spring display in a tub: yellow polyanthus with an edging of blue muscari (grape hyacinth). This arrangement is suitable for a position with light shade.

SPRING BEDDING PLANTS

To herald the spring what better than tubs and window boxes filled with polyanthus (*Primula polyantha*) with their large heads of flowers in shades of blue, red, pink, yellow and white? Polyanthus are also recommended for mass planting in small beds. This is the way we use polyanthus in Britain, but in the USA they are grown as pot plants.

Polyanthus like a moisture-retentive soil so containers are best filled with one of the peat-based potting composts. This is more moisture-retentive than soil-based composts.

Polyanthus can either be grown alone or mixed with miniature spring-flowering bulbs (see pp. 37–39). There are not many bulbs suited to shade but one that will succeed is muscari (grape hyacinth) with spikes of blue flowers. This looks lovely with yellow polyanthus (Fig. 10).

This corner is quietly furnished with *Alchemilla mollis* and buttercup-flowered trollius against a background of ivy and brought to life by a dazzling bowl of 'Yellow Crystal' violas.

Myosotis sylvatica (forget-me-not) is one of the most widely planted spring bedding plants, valued for its clouds of tiny blue flowers. It makes a marvellous underplanting for tulips, although unfortunately these bulbs will not grow in shade. However, try forget-me-nots with polyanthus, in tubs, window boxes or even hanging baskets. Forget-me-nots also need a moisture-retentive compost.

Winter-flowering pansies (varieties of *Viola* × *wittrockiana*) look lovely planted in hanging baskets, but they are also suited to any other type of container. They bloom in the depths of winter and continue into spring – a truly long flowering season. Well-known varieties are 'Floral Dance' and 'Universal', both offering a wide range of colours. Pansies also need a moisture-retentive compost and can be arranged with polyanthus and forget-me-nots if desired.

SUMMER BEDDING PLANTS

Among the most useful summer bedding plants for shade are the varieties of *Impatiens wallerana* (busy lizzie). These dwarf compact plants come in a wide range of colours, including shades of red, pink, orange and white. The plants bloom continuously from early summer until the start of frosts in autumn. They make a particularly fine show in hanging baskets, as well as in other containers and small beds and they relish moisture-retentive soil. In containers grow them in peat-based compost and keep well watered.

Impatiens really do not need any other plants with them, but if you want to create height in a planting scheme, use the foliage plant *Ricinus communis* (see below).

Another very useful flowering plant for shade is *Begonia semperflorens* (wax begonia), ideal for all kinds of containers or beds. The dwarf bushy plants with waxy green or bronze foliage smother themselves with red, pink or white flowers from early summer until the start of the autumn frosts. Moisture-retentive soil is required so use peat-based composts in containers.

A fairly new summer bedding subject is *Mimulus* × *hybridus* (monkey flower) with several flushes of trumpet-shaped blooms in shades of red, pink, orange and yellow throughout the summer. Mimulus are especially good for hanging baskets. However, they need plenty of moisture so should be grown in peat-based compost and watered well in dry weather. Cut off the dead blooms regularly to encourage more to follow.

There are several summer bedding plants which are often combined with the main subject to act as a contrast. For example, *Alyssum maritimum* (syn. *Lobularia maritima*) (sweet alyssum) is often used for edging beds or planting around the edges of tubs, window boxes and hanging baskets. It produces a carpet of white flowers throughout summer. There are also pink, rose-red and violet-purple varieties. It will not flower quite so freely in shade but nevertheless makes an acceptable display.

Lobelia erinus (lobelia) has similar uses to alyssum. It is popular in Britain but the summers in the USA tend to be too hot for it. There are both compact and trailing varieties of lobelia. The former are ideal for edging beds, while the latter are better for hanging baskets and the edges of containers. Lobelia is often combined with alyssum. Most varieties have blue flowers (they come in all shades) but there are pink, red and white shades available, too. Flowering might not be quite so good if the site is in shade all day long, but part shade is perfectly acceptable. Do not let lobelia dry out as it likes reasonably moist soil.

Cineraria maritima (silver-leaved cineraria) is generally used as a 'dot plant' in beds and containers to give height and, more importantly, contrast in shape and colour. It has deeply cut, lobed, silvery-grey leaves. It will not be quite so robust in shade as in full sun but nevertheless will grow reasonably well. It is best to cut off any flowers that are produced as they are not particularly attractive.

Another plant with similar uses is *Coleus blumei* (flame nettle), which has multicoloured nettle-like leaves. There are lots of varieties in many different colour combinations. Again cut off any flowers that are produced.

Also used as a dot plant is *Atriplex hortensis rubra* (orach), basically a foliage plant with crimson leaves, capable of reaching a height of at least 1.2 m (4 ft). Another popular foliage plant is *Ricinus communis* (castor oil plant), with large green palmate leaves, or bronze in some varieties. This is also a tallish plant, at least 1.2 m (4 ft) in height. All parts of this plant are poisonous (including the seeds).

Do not be afraid to try other summer bedding plants in shade as you may be surprised at the results. For instance, I was pleasantly surprised when I tried some zonal pelargoniums in my porch which receives no sun at all. They managed a modest display of flowers during the summer.

Remember that all of these summer bedding plants are tender and raised under glass in the spring. They should not be planted out until all danger of frost is over.

HARDY ANNUALS

These are sown direct into containers or beds in the spring and the seedlings thinned out to the correct spacing.

The majority of hardy annuals need a sunny position but the following

Not all windowboxes demand a position in full sun. This colourful display of impatiens and variegated ivy prefers the shady side of a house.

Exotic-looking lilies are woodland plants, so they enjoy a cool, moist root-run. Hence a potful like this will almost certainly last longer in bloom when kept out of direct sun.

will succeed in shade or partial shade, provided it is not too heavy.

If you like grassy plants try *Briza maxima* (greater quaking grass), ideal for patio beds. It has fresh green foliage and silvery brownish blooms. Height 60 cm (2 ft); thin out to 15–20 cm (6–8 in). *Euphorbia marginata* (snow on the mountain) is also recommended for patio beds. It is a bushy plant with bright green, white-edged foliage bracts at the top. The flowers, which are surrounded by these bracts, are insignificant. Height 60 cm (2 ft); thin out to 30 cm (12 in).

Ionopsidium acaule (violet cress) is one of the smallest hardy annuals and suitable for small containers and edging beds. Only 5–8 cm (2–3 in) high, and needing thinning to 10 cm (4 in), it produces masses of tiny four-petalled pale blue flowers in summer. This is actually a shade-loving plant and needs a moisture-retentive soil. Sow seeds in succession, up until mid-summer.

Lunaria annua (syn. *L. biennis*) (honesty) is actually a biennial: it is sown in late spring and flowers mid-spring/early summer the following year. The scented purple flowers are followed by large, rounded, silvery seed pods which are often dried for winter flower arranging. Suitable for a patio bed. Height 75–90 cm ($2\frac{1}{2}$–3 ft); spacing 30 cm (12 in).

A well-loved and easily grown annual for small beds and containers is *Malcolmia maritima* (Virginian stock). It comes in a mixture of colours including shades of pink, lilac, red, cream and white. The tiny four-petalled flowers are carried on thin stems. Best to make two sowings: early spring and mid-summer. Height 15 cm (6 in); thin out to 15 cm.

Of similar stature to Virginian stock is *Nemophila menziesii* (syn. *N. insignis*) (baby blue eyes), with the most beautiful blue, white-centred flowers set against pale green feathery foliage. Use in containers or for edging beds.

Omphalodes linifolia (Venus's navelwort) is not too well-known but is a delightful little annual rather like a white-flowered myosotis (forget-me-not). Ideal for edging a bed. Height up to 30 cm (12 in); thin out to 20 cm (8 in).

Ideal for edging small beds, for gaps in paving or for tubs is *Phacelia campanularia* (Californian bluebell), with pure blue bell-shaped flowers. Height 22 cm (9 in); thin out to 15 cm (6 in).

Varieties of *Tropaeolum majus* (nasturtium) grow quite well in shade and their large showy flowers come in shades of red, pink, yellow and orange. There are dwarf bushy varieties, around 30 cm (12 in) in height and spread, and climbing kinds up to 1.8 m (6 ft) in height, ideal for a shady wall or fence. The dwarf kinds are excellent for tubs, window boxes and hanging baskets.

BULBS

There are not too many bulbs which will thrive in shade. I have given a selection in Chapter 3 and any of these could be grown in patio beds or even in containers such as tubs.

Some lilies are excellent in tubs, particularly *Lilium regale* (regal lily) with large white trumpet-shaped flowers, which are deliciously scented, in mid-summer. Height 1.2–1.8 m (4–6 ft). When grown in a tub it can be kept in a sunny spot, which it really prefers, until it is coming into flower, when it can be transferred to the shady patio or courtyard. You should be able to get three bulbs in a 30 cm (12 in) diameter pot or tub. Plant them well down in soil-based potting compost, in autumn.

Miniature narcissus (daffodils) are excellent for containers and small patio beds and they relish shade, provided it is not too heavy, or partial shade, and moisture-retentive (but not wet) soil. There are many miniature species, like *N. asturiensis* (syn. *N. minimus*), with yellow trumpet-shaped flowers in late winter. Height 8 cm (3 in). *N. bulbocodium* (hoop petticoat daffodil) has flared trumpet-shaped yellow flowers in late winter/early spring. Height up to 15 cm (6 in). *N. cyclamineus* is a delightful little species, each flower having a long 'trumpet' and swept-back petals. The colour is deep yellow. Height about 15 cm (6 in). *N. triandrus albus* (angel's tears) has creamy-white blooms in spring and grows to about 10 cm (4 in) in height.

The ideal position for these little daffodils is one which receives dappled shade from trees. Plant them in bold groups, during autumn, spacing the bulbs 8 cm (3 in) apart and 8 cm deep.

CHAPTER 7

LAWNS IN SHADE

Creating a lawn in shade is often not as difficult as some people imagine. In light shade, for example that created by tall buildings or screens with the site open to the sky, you should obtain reasonable growth of all grasses which are used for lawns.

You should obtain a reasonably good lawn in the dappled shade of small trees which have a light canopy of foliage.

The heavier the shade, though, the more difficult it becomes to establish a lawn and it may therefore be better to resort to suitable ground-cover plants.

The most difficult situation is found under certain trees – for example, large oaks or beeches create very deep shade and it is unlikely that grass will grow beneath them.

There are other problems under trees, too, especially large trees: they take moisture and nutrients from the soil in large quantities, leaving little or none for the grass. The lawn becomes sparse and is then invaded by moss and other weeds. So under large trees casting heavy shade, where the soil is poor and dry, I again suggest opting for some of the highly tolerant ground-cover shrubs and perennials.

I write from experience: in my lawn there is a large mature beech tree. Originally the lawn was laid right up to the trunk; now under the branch spread it is simply a carpet of moss, which in fact looks quite attractive. I may well leave it at that, at least for a few years until I get round to planning and planting this area. In another part of the garden I have successfully established a grass bank in the dappled shade cast by birch trees and large shrubs. I used an 'ordinary' grass-seed mixture formulated for fine ornamental lawns and I keep the grass semi-long, cutting it only a few times during the growing season with an electric nylon-cord trimmer. There are, however, grass-seed mixtures specially formulated for shady areas which contain a number of different grasses, all tolerant of shady conditions. Let's take a look at them.

CHOOSING SUITABLE GRASSES

A typical grass-seed mixture might contain rough-stalked meadow grass

A lawn is likely to remain greener in summer when shaded by trees, provided their roots do not rob the soil of too much moisture.

(*Poa trivialis*), wood meadow grass (*Poa nemoralis*) and creeping red fescue (*Festuca rubra rubra*).

The mixture will almost certainly contain a high proportion of rough-stalked meadow grass, a tufted species spreading by short stolons. It has deep green foliage, which is dull above and shiny below. It grows best in moist rich soil and should not be mown too closely (certainly no closer than 19 mm ($\frac{3}{4}$ in).

Wood meadow grass is also a tufted species, with very narrow, soft, deep green foliage. It takes deep shade and thrives in damp soil but must not be mown too often or you will eradicate it.

Creeping red fescue has a creeping habit, spreads by rhizomes and has rather bristly leaves. This grass tolerates drought conditions but not very close mowing. It grows best in light sandy soil although it is very adaptable as regards soils, growing equally well in moist conditions.

Another grass species that takes shade well, if not cut too hard, is fine-leaved fescue (*Festuca tenuifolia*). It has extremely fine thin foliage. Particularly suitable for dry soils, this grass may also be included in some shade-tolerant seed mixtures.

You will notice that these grasses should not be mown too closely; so a lawn in shade must be mown less frequently than one in sun and is therefore allowed to grow longer. When you do mow, do not cut it hard – no lower than about 2.5 cm (1 in).

SPECIAL MAINTENANCE REQUIREMENTS

I have already mentioned that the grasses forming a shady lawn should be allowed to grow longer than those forming a lawn in sun. Also, you will need to carry out a regular feeding programme, particularly if the lawn is under trees. The tree roots will take a lot of nutrients in the growing season.

Two feeds are recommended each year: one in the spring, using a proprietary lawn fertilizer formulated for spring/summer use, and another in the autumn, again using a proprietary lawn fertilizer formulated for that season.

Watering is very important if the soil is inclined to dry out in warm weather. Under trees regular watering, at least once a week, is essential in dry weather. Tree roots take an incredible amount of moisture from the soil during the growing season. You should use a lawn sprinkler and apply enough water for it to penetrate the soil to a depth of at least 15 cm (6 in).

Under trees it is especially important to carry out aeration in the autumn, by spiking the lawn with a garden fork to a depth of about

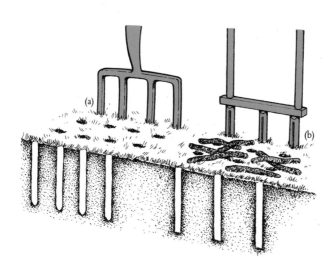

Fig. 11 Under trees it is especially important to aerate the lawn. This is best done in the autumn. The lawn is spiked with a garden fork *(a)*; but very wet soil can be aerated with a hollow-tined fork *(b)* and the holes filled with sandy compost. This type of fork takes out cores of soil.

15 cm (6 in) (Fig. 11a). This allows moisture and nutrients to penetrate more easily. Carry out spiking in the summer, too, if you feel that water is simply running off the surface rather than penetrating the soil.

Weeds can appear in any lawn but there are some which are typical of shady areas, like *Ranunculus ficaria* (lesser celandine). This does not succumb readily to lawn weedkillers, so several applications may be needed in the spring and summer.

Mosses are often troublesome in shady lawns and, contrary to popular belief, they are remarkably drought resistant so are capable of establishing under trees. Mosses are also encouraged by compacted soil, wet conditions at the soil surface, lack of nutrients and acid conditions, so try to correct these problems. Compacted or very wet soil can be improved by aeration as described above. In the latter case use a hollow-tined fork and fill the resultant holes with a sandy compost to assist drainage (Fig. 11b). This should be done in the autumn. A suitable compost consists of four parts sand, two parts loam and one part peat (parts by volume). Brush the mix into the holes formed by hollow-tining.

Lack of nutrients can only be rectified by regular feeding, of course, as outlined above. If the soil is very acid, with a pH of below 5.5 (determine this by testing the soil with one of the proprietary soil-testing kits) then you should apply carbonate of lime, such as ground limestone, in the autumn, at a rate of 56g per sq metre (2 oz per sq yd).

Moss can be eradicated by applying a proprietary mosskiller or lawn sand in the spring, according to the maker's instructions. When the moss is dead (it will turn black) rake it out with a wire lawn rake. Never rake out live moss as you will only spread it and make matters worse.

Algae can appear in shady conditions with moist soil, creating black slippery patches. Algae are primitive simple plants and can be eradicated with a mosskiller or lawn sand. Aerating and topdressing in autumn as described above will help to prevent algae from becoming established.

Lichens may also appear in the shady lawn. These are primitive plants consisting of a combination of an alga and a fungus, which live together in mutual harmony. Lichens are not particularly serious on the lawn, invading sparse turf resulting from poor growing conditions and drainage. These conditions should be improved to keep lichens at bay. Eliminate them with lawn sand or lawn mosskiller. The most common lichen consists of leaf-like growths which are brownish or blackish when moist, but greyish when dry, when the 'leaves' also curl to reveal their undersides, which are white in colour. Lichens are invariably found in lawns under trees.

CHAPTER 8

SPECIAL FEATURES

Every garden should have one or two special features, ideally devoted to a collection of choice or desirable plants to create an air of individuality. Those described in this chapter should certainly appeal to the keen plantsman/gardener, are guaranteed to interest your garden-loving visitors and will give you a great deal of pleasure through the seasons.

Only a fortunate few are able to create a woodland garden, although there is no reason why a mini-woodland should not be a feature of a medium-sized garden. A garden of any size can accommodate a peat bed with a collection of dwarf rhododendrons and other lime-hating plants; and likewise a rock garden. A shaded rock garden makes an ideal home for many choice alpine plants. Again, only a fortunate few have a natural stream running through their garden, although artificial streams, linking garden pools, are becoming popular. The moist streamside with dappled shade is the perfect setting for many moisture-loving and bog plants.

We are in the midst of a conservatory revolution and there have probably never been so many homes that boast a 'garden room'. Although the conservatory should ideally receive plenty of sun, this is not always possible. But a shady conservatory can certainly be 'furnished' with a collection of flowering and foliage plants.

WOODLAND GARDEN

An area of woodland is a feature of many large gardens, especially those in rural areas, although there is no reason why a mini-woodland garden should not be created in a medium-sized town or suburban garden to form a refreshing oasis.

Dense woodland with deep shade, such as that formed of large mature beech trees (fagus) is no good for creating a woodland garden as few of the woodland plants would thrive. Either an area is thinned out to let in more light or you leave the woodland completely natural, with mosses and the few native plants that will bear the dense shade.

The ideal woodland garden has well-spaced trees creating dappled shade. The crowns of trees should not be touching – there should be space between them for sunlight to penetrate.

STARTING FROM SCRATCH

If you decide to plant an area of woodland you should choose trees that are reasonably fast growing and which have a light airy crown of branches and foliage. Even a group of, say, three such trees will create an ideal area for woodland plants.

Choose the smaller-growing trees, such as *Betula pendula* (common silver birch), or birches with whiter bark, such as *B. jacquemontii, B. papyrifera, B. ermanii* or *B. platyphylla szechuanica*. There are several other small trees which could be mixed with these birches, such as *Sorbus aucuparia* (mountain ash) and its varieties; *Sorbus aria* (whitebeam); *Prunus avium* (gean); *Prunus padus* (bird cherry); *Prunus subhirtella* 'Autumnalis' (autumn cherry); and *Prunus serrula* (an ornamental cherry).

Plant these trees 7.5–9 m (25–30 ft) apart each way. This will give them plenty of space to develop properly without growing into each other.

Beaten-earth paths meandering through the woodland will naturally divide it into irregular-shaped beds for planting. These beds should be well dug, at the same time incorporating as much leafmould, pulverized bark or peat as you can afford, for many woodland plants like a humus-rich soil. These materials will also help to conserve moisture – particularly important if you have a light sandy well-drained soil.

Finances permitting, the paths could be covered with a coarse grade of pulverized bark. Alternatively you might like 'stepping-stone' paths formed of 15 cm (6 in) thick tree-trunk sections sunk into the ground so that their tops are level with the surrounding soil. First, though, treat them with a horticultural wood preservative to prolong their life.

Next you should decide on a theme for your woodland garden – it could be an English or exotic woodland.

ENGLISH WOODLAND GARDEN

Here the 'framework' of the planting scheme could consist of evergreen shrubs: *Ilex aquifolium* (holly); *Taxus baccata* (yew); and *Daphne laureola* (spurge laurel).

Space these out well, and then plant between them bold groups and drifts of such typically English woodland plants as *Anemone nemorosa* (windflower); *Primula vulgaris* (primrose); *Endymion non-scriptus* (bluebell); and *Narcissus pseudonarcissus* (wild daffodil or lent lily). All of these are spring-flowering. For early summer I suggest bold groups of *Digitalis purpurea* (wild foxglove), and to follow these, drifts of *Meconopsis cambrica* (Welsh poppy).

Winter is never dull in an English woodland garden, with its attractive evergreen shrubs which then really come into their own, but further interest can be provided by planting bold drifts of *Galanthus nivalis* (snowdrop) and *Helleborus foetidus* (stinking hellebore).

EXOTIC WOODLAND GARDEN

An exotic woodland garden is more colourful and flamboyant than the 'cool and restful' English woodland. Bear in mind that some of the plants recommended need an acid or lime-free soil and this is indicated as appropriate.

As with the English woodland garden we should have a 'framework' of shrubs. If you have acid soil the natural choice is the rhododendron tribe. This is a vast genus, so much so that it is difficult to know what to recommend. However, the hardy hybrids are very popular, making a magnificent show of colour in spring/early summer and, as the name implies, they are very hardy. Well-known varieties are 'Britannia' (crimson), 'Christmas Cheer' (white), 'Doncaster' (crimson), 'Fastuosum Flore Pleno' (mauve), 'Gomer Waterer' (white and mauve), 'Mrs G. W. Leak' (rose-pink), 'Pink Pearl' (lilac-pink), 'Purple Splendour' (deep purple) and 'Sappho' (white and purple).

Deciduous azaleas can provide vibrant colour in late spring/early summer, as can the dwarf evergreen azaleas which are ideal for the edges of beds. (Azaleas are strictly rhododendrons).

There are many species of rhododendron, such as *R. augustinii*, a large shrub with blue flowers; *R. fictolacteum*, a large-leaved small tree with white flowers; *R. mucronulatum*, deciduous, purple flowers in winter; and *R. wardii*, large shrub with light yellow flowers.

Camellias are excellent woodland shrubs and all are evergreen. Only suitable for acid soils. They flower in winter or spring and should be protected from early-morning sun which can damage frozen flower buds. There are literally hundreds of varieties of *Camellia japonica* but very popular are 'Adolphe Audusson' (rich red) and 'Lady Clare' (deep pink). Highly recommended are the *C.* × *williamsii* varieties, particularly 'Donation' with large semi-double bright pink flowers.

An unusual deciduous shrub for acid soils is *Enkianthus campanulatus* with cream bell-shaped flowers in spring. The evergreen *Kalmia latifolia* also needs acid soil and in early summer produces clusters of flowers the colour of pink icing sugar.

The evergreen pieris must have acid soil and produce, in spring, trusses of white bell-shaped flowers. Some are noted for their brilliant red new foliage, particularly 'Forest Flame' and *P. formosa forrestii*.

For autumn foliage colour in the exotic woodland garden there is nothing to beat the varieties of *Acer palmatum* (Japanese maple). They will grow in alkaline soil but must have protection from cold winds and early morning sun. One of the best varieties is *A.p.* 'Heptalobum Osakazuki'.

Magnolias are at home in woodland. Choose those which flower at an early age, like *M. × soulangiana* and its varieties, and *M. stellata*. They flower in the spring and are deciduous.

All of these shrubs used to form the 'framework' of planting schemes eventually form medium-sized to large bushes and need moisture-retentive soil – do not allow the soil to dry out.

BULBS AND PERENNIALS

There is a wealth of choice bulbs and perennials which can be planted within the framework of shrubs, ideally in bold groups and drifts. Here's a selection.

Anemone (windflower)
Anemone blanda has blue, pink or white blooms in spring. Height 15 cm (6 in); plant 10 cm (4 in) apart.

Brunnera
In spring/early summer *B. macrophylla* produces clouds of blue myosotis-like flowers. Height and spread 45 cm (18 in).

Cyclamen
C. hederifolium (syn. *C. neapolitanum*) is a hardy miniature cyclamen with silver-marbled foliage and pink or white flowers in autumn. Height and spread 10 cm (4 in). Tolerates dry soil.

Eranthis (winter aconite)
Growing from tubers, *E. hyemalis* produces yellow flowers in late winter/early spring. Best in moisture-retentive soil. Height 10 cm (4 in); plant 8 cm (3 in) apart.

Erythronium (dog's tooth violet)
Bulbous plants, of which *E. dens-canis* is the best known, with pink lily-like flowers in spring and bronze-marbled foliage. Height and spread 15 cm (6 in). Must have moisture-retentive soil.

Fritillaria (fritillary)
There are many species of these bulbous plants, but try the popular *F. meleagris* (snake's head fritillary) with pendulous, bell-shaped, purple or white flowers in spring. Most have a subtle all-over chequerboard marking on their bells. This is now a very rare native plant. Height 30 cm (12 in); plant 10 cm (4 in) apart.

This corner of a wild garden is crammed with colour and interest during spring from bluebells and forget-me-nots interspersed with the delicate foliage of Japanese maples and ferns.

Geranium (crane's bill)
Easy-going herbaceous plants flowering profusely in summer. Try
G. pratense with blue flowers, height and spread about 60 cm (2 ft);
G. phaeum, blackish-purple flowers, height and spread about 60 cm (2 ft);
and *G. sanguineum*, reddish-purple, height 20 cm (8 in), spread 45 cm
(18 in).

Lilium (lily)
A vast genus of bulbs and marvellous companions for rhododendrons.
Plant them in bold drifts or groups. Easy to grow are the mid-century
hybrids like orange-red 'Enchantment' and yellow 'Destiny'. Height is
about 60 cm (2 ft); plant 15 cm (6 in) apart in moisture-retentive, humus-
rich soil.

Meconopsis
The blue poppies like *M. betonicifolia*, height 90 cm (3 ft), spread 45 cm
(18 in), and *M. grandis*, height and spread 60 cm (2 ft), flower in summer
but they are rather short-lived perennials, needing moisture-retentive
soil.

Mertensia
M. virginica (Virginian cowslip) is a perennial with clusters of bell-shaped
blue flowers in spring. Height and spread about 30 cm (12 in). Best in
moist soil.

Polygonatum (Solomon's seal)
Herbaceous perennials with dangling bell-shaped white flowers in spring/
early summer. *P. × hybridum* is usually grown; height 60–90 cm (2–3 ft),
spread 30–45 cm (12–18 in). Provide humus-rich soil.

Primula
This is a very large genus, but for the woodland garden I can recommend
P. denticulata (drumstick primrose) with globular heads of mauve, blue,
purple, pink, red or white flowers in spring. Height and spread 30 cm
(12 in). Also try some of the summer-flowering candelabra primulas with
tiers of flowers on tall stems, like *P. japonica* in shades of red, pink or
white. Height 60 cm (2 ft), spread 30 cm (12 in). Primulas need moisture-
retentive soil.

Saxifraga (saxifrage)
S. fortunei is a herbaceous perennial with heads of white starry flowers in
autumn. Height and spread about 30 cm (12 in). Likes cool moist soil.

Trillium

These are herbaceous perennials with showy three-petalled flowers in spring or early summer. Well-known is *T. grandiflorum* (wake robin) with white blooms. Height and spread about 30 cm (12 in). Moist humus-rich soil needed.

PEAT BEDS

If you have a cool shady spot in the garden (including dappled shade cast by trees), consider a peat bed for lime-hating plants (Fig. 12). This is possible even if you have limy or alkaline soil, for the bed is raised above soil level and filled with a lime-free compost.

Fig. 12 A section of a raised peat bed, built up with peat blocks and filled with lime-free compost. There are many plants which can be grown in this bed, such as *Cassiope lycopodioides (left)* with white bell-shaped flowers in spring; and dwarf rhododendrons, both large-flowered hybrids (*right*) and small-flowered species.

The bed can be any shape or size but should have a minimum depth of 30 cm (12 in); preferably 45 cm (18 in) if your garden soil is limy. The bed is built up with peat blocks – brick-sized blocks of compressed peat. First moisten them thoroughly by soaking in water for 24 hours. Then build the walls of the bed, staggering the blocks like bricks in a wall. The joints are filled with the same compost that is used for filling the beds. Make the walls tilt slightly inwards for stability.

When you have built up the walls to the required height place an 8 cm (3 in) deep layer of coarse peat over the soil and then fill the bed with acid or lime-free compost, consisting of: 4 parts moist sphagnum peat, 1 part fibrous acid loam and 1 part lime-free coarse sand (parts by volume).

When planting is complete, the surface of the bed is mulched with moist peat which should be topped up annually. The bed must never be allowed to dry out; nor must the peat blocks, otherwise they will shrink. So have a water sprinkler on hand during dry weather.

A CHOICE OF PLANTS
Cassiope
Dwarf evergreen shrubs with white bell-shaped flowers in spring. A well-known species is *C. lycopodioides*, 8 cm (3 in) high and spreading to 30–45 cm (12–18 in).

A typical English woodland association of primroses, bluebells and ferns can easily be imitated in a suitably moist shady part of a garden.

Cornus (dogwood)
The dwarf herbaceous perennial *C. canadensis* has showy white bracts surrounding the small greenish flowers which appear in early summer. height up to 15 cm (6 in); spread 60 cm (2 ft).

Gentiana (gentian)
Several gentians are suitable for peat beds including *G. acaulis* (trumpet gentian) with the most beautiful pure blue trumpet-shaped flowers in late spring/early summer. Height 8 cm (3 in); spread 30–45 cm (12–18 in).

Lithospermum
A somewhat shrubby prostrate plant, *L. diffusum* 'Heavenly Blue' also has true-blue flowers, produced from early summer to autumn. Height 8 cm (3 in); spread 60 cm (2 ft).

Parochetus
P. communis is a carpeting perennial, rather clover-like in general appearance but with bright blue pea-like flowers in summer and autumn. It is not reliably hardy in areas subject to hard winters. Height 8 cm (3 in); spread 60 cm (2 ft).

Philesia
The low-growing evergreen shrub *P. magellanica* produces red bell-shaped flowers in spring and early summer. Not recommended for areas subject to hard winters. Height 15 cm (6 in) or more; spread may be up to 90 cm (3 ft).

Phlox
P. adsurgens is a dwarf perennial with masses of warm pink flowers in summer. Height and spread 30 cm (12 in).

Phyllodoce
A carpeting evergreen shrub, *P. aleutica* bears clusters of yellowy-green flowers in spring and early summer. Rather heath-like in appearance; height 8 cm (3 in) or more; spread 30 cm (12 in).

Primula
There are some choice species in this genus for the peat bed. The following are dwarf primrose-like plants: *P. bhutanica*, pale blue yellow-eyed flowers in spring; *P. gracilipes* with attractive toothed leaves and deep pink green-yellow-eyed flowers in spring; and *P. whitei* with pastel-blue flowers in spring. These grow best in cool moist northern districts.

Rhododendron
Dwarf rhododendron species are ideal for the peat bed, like *R. impeditum* with purplish-blue flowers in spring, height 15 cm (6 in) or more, spread 60 cm (2 ft); and *R. scintillans*, violet-blue flowers in spring, height and spread at least 60 cm (2 ft). There are also many dwarf hybrid rhododendrons to choose from.

THE SHADY ROCK GARDEN

Rock gardens are generally built on a sunny site because the majority of alpines need plenty of sun. However, if such a site is not available one should not be put off creating a rock garden, as there is a good range of shade-loving or shade-tolerant rock plants. Even if the rock garden is in an open sunny position it may still have shaded areas, such as the north side, where the shade-lovers should be grown.

ROCK PLANTS FOR SHADE

Arabis
Varieties of *A. caucasica*, such as the double 'Flore Pleno' and the single 'Snowflake', both with masses of white blooms studding grey mats of foliage from late winter to early summer, are suitable for shaded areas. Height 20 cm (8 in); spread 60 cm (2 ft). The species itself is quite invasive and not recommended.

Campanula (bellflower)
Several species are suitable: *C. garganica*, *C. cochlearifolia*, *C. pulla* and *C. carpatica*, all with blue bell- or star-shaped flowers in summer. Height approximately 15 cm (6 in); spread 30 cm (12 in).

Corydalis
The species *C. lutea* has yellow tubular flowers in spring and summer set against ferny foliage. Height 15 cm (6 in); spread 30 cm (12 in).

Daphne
D. cneorum is a prostrate evergreen shrub with scented pink blooms in spring. Height 15 cm (6 in); spread at least 60 cm (2 ft).

Haberlea
These shade-loving rosette-forming perennials are ideal for shady crevices. They produce mauve-purple primula-like flowers in spring. Species include *H. ferdinandi-coburgii*, height 15 cm (6 in), spread 20 cm

(8 in); and the slightly smaller *H. rhodopensis*. They love leafy soil.

Hepatica

Hepaticas are also peat-loving perennial plants flowering in spring. Several species, perhaps the best-known being *H. nobilis* whose forms have single as well as double flowers in shades of purple, red, blue and white. Height 10 cm (4 in); spread 30 cm (12 in).

Iberis (perennial candytuft)

I. sempervirens and its varieties are shade-tolerant evergreens with white flowers in spring/early summer. Height 15–20 cm (6–8 in); spread 30–45 cm (12–18 in).

Phlox

P. adsurgens produces masses of warm pink blooms in summer. Height 30 cm (12 in); spread similar. Grow in cool peaty soil.

Primula

Several species are suitable for the shady rock garden, including *P. clarkei*, deep pink flowers, spring, height 5 cm (2 in), spread 15 cm (6 in); and *P. frondosa* with pinky-mauve flowers in spring, height and spread about 10 cm (4 in).

Ramonda

Evergreen perennials with a rosette-like habit, producing blue flowers in spring. Ideal for shady moist peaty crevices. Best-known species is *R. myconi*, height and spread about 15 cm (6 in).

Saxifraga (saxifrage)

Several are suitable for shady places like *S.* × *urbium* and its varieties, and the mossy saxifrages (species in the Dactyloides section). All are dwarf mat-forming plants which can spread to about 30 cm (12 in). They flower in spring.

Shortia

Evergreen perennials flowering in spring and revelling in acid peaty soil and shade. Best known is *S. uniflora* with pink, fringed flowers. Height 10 cm (4 in), spread 30 cm (12 in).

THE STREAMSIDE

Whilst I realize that only a lucky few have a natural stream running

The perimeter of woodland can be enlivened with the blooms of rhododendrons, foxgloves like the Excelsior hybrids, and long-spurred aquilegias.

A deep, permanently moist soil, together with a degree of shade to keep off the drying sun, are the secrets of this lush and colourful display of primulas, foxgloves and *Iris sibirica*.

through the garden, one should not dismiss the possibility of creating an artificial stream, linking two garden pools. Such schemes are relatively easy to achieve today, thanks to butyl-rubber pool liners.

The moist streamside, with dappled shade cast by a light canopy of tree foliage, is the perfect setting for many moisture-loving and bog plants. I can highly recommend the following.

A CHOICE OF PLANTS
Astilbe
Hardy perennials with feathery plumes of flowers in summer, needing soil which is permanently moist. Popular are varieties of *A.* × *arendsii* with pink, red or white flowers. Height up to 90 cm (3 ft), spread 30–45 cm (12–18 in).

Caltha (marsh marigold)
The double marsh marigold, *C. palustris* 'Plena', with deep yellow flowers in spring, is ideal for planting in wet soil at the water's edge. Height about 15 cm (6 in), spread 30 cm (12 in).

Iris
Waterside irises include *I. laevigata* with dark blue flowers in early summer, height 60 cm (2 ft), spread 45 cm (18 in); and *I. pseudacorus*, yellow flowers during same period, height up to 1.2 m (4 ft), spread 60 cm (2 ft).

Ligularia
Several herbaceous perennial species suitable for moisture-retentive soil including *L. clivorum* with large dramatic foliage and heads of deep yellow daisy-like flowers in summer, height and spread at least 90 cm (3 ft); *L. przewalskii*, bold spikes of yellow daisy flowers in summer, height up to 1.8 m (6 t), spread 90 cm (3 ft); and *L. tangutica* with plume-like heads of yellow blooms in early autumn, height about 1.8 m (6 ft), spread 90 cm (3 ft).

Lysichitum (skunk cabbage)
A truly dramatic herbaceous perennial for wet soil, *L. americanum* has large yellow sail-like flowers in early spring, before the huge lush leaves appear. Height 60–90 cm (2–3 ft), spread 60 cm (2 ft).

Lythrum
Herbaceous perennials for moist or wet positions, producing spikes of flowers in summer. Varieties of two species are grown: *L. salicaria*, such as 'Robert' and 'The Beacon', with pinkish-red flowers; and *L. virgatum*,

particularly 'The Rocket' and 'Rose Queen' in bright pink. Height around 90 cm (3 ft), spread 45 cm (18 in).

Mimulus (monkey flower)

These perennials are rather short-lived and thrive in wet soils, making a bright show of colour in summer with their often spotted flowers. Species include *M. cardinalis*, red and yellow flowers, height up to 60 cm (2 ft), spread 30 cm (12 in); *M. cupreus*, bronzy-orange, brown-spotted flowers, height and spread 30 cm (12 in); and *M. luteus*, yellow, crimson-spotted flowers, height variable, from 15–60 cm (6–24 in), spread 30 cm (12 in).

Osmunda (royal fern)

A stately waterside fern up to 1.5 m (5 ft) in height with fresh green fronds which take on autumn tints. Appreciates plenty of humus in the soil.

Primula

There are quite a few moisture-loving primulas for the streamside, including the diminutive *P. rosea* with bright pink flowers in spring; height and spread up to 15 cm (6 in). Taller primulas, summer flowering, include *P. japonica* with whorls of red flowers, height 60 cm (2 ft), spread 30 cm (12 in); the crimson *P. pulverulenta* with whorls of flowers on 90 cm (3 ft) stems, spread 30 cm (12 in); *P. sikkimensis* (Himalayan cowslip), light yellow scented blooms, height 45 cm (18 in), spread 30 cm (12 in); *P. florindae* (giant cowslip), globular heads of light yellow, scented flowers, can attain 1.8 m (6 ft) in height, spread 45 cm (18 in); *P. beesiana*, whorls of purplish flowers, height 60 cm (2 ft), spread 30 cm (12 in); and *P. bulleyana*, pale orange blooms in tiers, height up to 90 cm (3 ft), spread 30 cm (12 in).

Rodgersia

Herbaceous perennials for moist soil, valued for their dramatic foliage. *R. aesculifolia* has bronze hand-shaped leaves, height up to 1.8 m (6 ft), spread 90 cm (3 ft); *R. pinnata* 'Superba' is somewhat similar but half the height; and *R. tabularis* has large green parasol-shaped leaves, height and spread 90 cm (3 ft). All produce feathery flowers in summer.

Trollius (globe flower)

Herbaceous perennials with mainly yellow or orange globular flowers in late spring/early summer. Hybrids are normally grown (*T. × hybridus*) like 'Canary Bird' and the orangy-yellow 'Orange Princess'. Height up

A few alpine plants actually prefer the shady side of an outcrop. *Ramonda pyrenaica* will thrive in a cool, moist crevice.

to 75 cm (2½ ft), spread 45 cm (18 in). Must be grown in moist soil.

THE SHADED CONSERVATORY

Although the conservatory or 'garden room' should ideally be sited against a sunny wall, this is not always possible. Fortunately, though, there is a range of flowering and foliage plants which will flourish in

Some of our most treasured pot plants – notably begonias, primulas and cyclamen – grow and bloom more lustily when shaded from the full force of the sun.

shady conditions. I will concentrate on those for the cool conservatory, with a minimum temperature of 7°C (45°F), which is what most people maintain.

FLOWERING PLANTS

Pots of wax begonias, *Begonia semperflorens*, will make a good display during the summer and should be raised annually from seeds.

Camellias can be grown as permanent pot plants and varieties of *C. japonica* and *C.* × *williamsii* bloom in the winter and spring. Also winter-flowering is the Indian azalea, *Rhododendron simsii*.

Winter and spring colour can also be provided by primulas, such as *P. obconica, P. malacoides* and *P.* × *kewensis*, as well as coloured primroses and polyanthus. All are raised from seeds each year. Also seed-raised annually are cinerarias (*Senecio* × *hybridus*) which bloom in late winter and spring.

Several of the bellflowers or campanulas can be recommended for summer flowering, particularly *C. pyramidalis* (chimney bellflower) with spikes of blue or white flowers. This is a biennial, raised each year from seeds. *C. isophylla* is a perennial of trailing habit, ideal for hanging baskets, and produces blue or white starry flowers.

Greenhouse fuchsias should perform reasonably well in the shady conservatory during the summer, as should impatiens (busy Lizzie), the latter being raised annually from seeds.

Pots of hydrangeas will bloom well, in spring or summer, and are best replaced regularly with young plants raised from spring cuttings.

Streptocarpus hybrids will bloom all summer. They are evergreen perennials and can be kept from year to year.

FOLIAGE PLANTS

A favourite foliage plant for the conditions under discussion is *Aspidistra elatior* (cast-iron plant) with large deep green leaves. It is a long-lived perennial.

Various ferns will thrive, such as *Asplenium bulbiferum* (spleenwort), *Cyrtomium falcatum* (holly fern), and *Pellaea rotundifolia* (cliffbrake). Hedera (ivies) can be grown as trailers or climbers. Choose varieties of *H. helix*; or *H. canariensis* 'Variegata' (variegated Canary Island ivy).

Chlorophytum comosum 'Variegatum' (spider plants) will thrive, and so, too, will the climbers *Cissus antarctica* and *Rhoicissus rhomboidea* (grape ivy).

CHAPTER 9

THE BONES OF THE GARDEN

Of course most gardens do not consist entirely of plants but have a basic permanent framework or structure (the 'bones' of the garden) such as paved areas, paths, walling, fencing and so on, all helping to form a number of areas, each hopefully with its own particular 'atmosphere', which are then furnished with plants.

Further atmosphere is created with statuary and other ornaments, and an idea that is gaining in popularity is the use of mirrors on walls, etc, to create illusions of extra depth in the garden.

Here we look at all of this garden 'hardware' in relation to shady gardens, or shaded areas: considering suitable materials and how to maintain them.

CONSTRUCTION MATERIALS

In a shaded area one should try to use light-coloured materials for paving, walling, etc, as they help to lighten the area by reflecting light.

If you want to construct a patio, terrace or path you will find that there is a wide range of pre-cast concrete paving slabs in garden centres these days. Many come in light colours, such as pale grey, pastel greens and natural stone colours, as well as white. All of these colours will effectively reflect light and brighten a shady part of the garden.

An alternative to paving slabs for patios, terraces and paths is gravel, in the form of pea shingle which is readily available from builders' merchants. Pea shingle consists of fingernail-sized stones, and overall is very light in colour: it contains shades of white, buff, beige etc. Unlike paving slabs gravel is very quick and easy to lay: simply spread a 2.5– 5 cm (1–2 in) layer over well-rammed soil and retain the edges with strips of timber or mini curb stones.

Pea shingle goes with any style of architecture or garden – traditional or modern.

Timber can be used for paths in some situations, particularly in natural parts of the garden and in woodland gardens. Sections of tree trunk, 15 cm (6 in) thick, can be sunk into the ground so that their tops are level with the surrounding soil. Place them in the form of stepping stones. It is best to treat the sections with a horticultural wood preservative before installing them (after removing the bark) as this prolongs their life.

Ornamental garden walling can be built with concrete walling blocks. Again these are generally very light in colour, often in natural stone colours. Brick walling is oten too dark for shady areas unless mellow, yellow bricks are used.

Screen-block walling (concerete blocks with an openwork pattern) is very light in colour and generally used to form screens in the garden or around a patio.

Dark gloomy corners formed of, say, high boundary walls can often be improved by painting the walls a light colour, using white, cream or a light pastel-coloured masonry paint. If the walls are old it is best to first seal them by applying a masonry stabilizing solution. When dry this results in a hard dust-free surface which is then painted.

One has little choice of light-coloured fencing for brightening up shady areas. The most obvious example is timber ranch-type fencing painted white (Fig. 13a). This consists of horizontal boards, with gaps between them, nailed to vertical posts. Ranch-type fencing is often used for boundaries in modern gardens.

For country gardens paling or picket fencing, again painted white, makes a good boundary (Fig. 13b). Usually 1–1.2 m (3–4 ft) high, it is constructed of narrow vertical strips of timber (pointed or rounded at the top) spaced approximately 8 cm (3 in) apart, nailed to horizontal members supported by fencing posts.

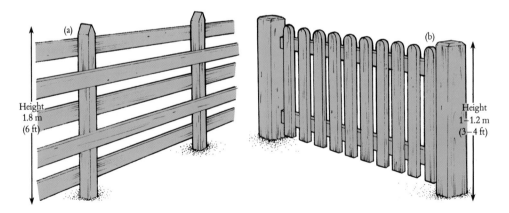

Fig. 13 Types of fencing, both of which can be painted white to lighten up a shady area. (*a*) Timber ranch-type fencing, often used for boundaries in modern gardens. (*b*) Paling or picket fencing, which makes an attractive boundary in country gardens.

To divide the garden internally, consider timber trellis screens painted white. Both modern and traditional styles are available (Fig. 14), but some you may have to paint yourself as they come treated with natural-coloured wood preservatives.

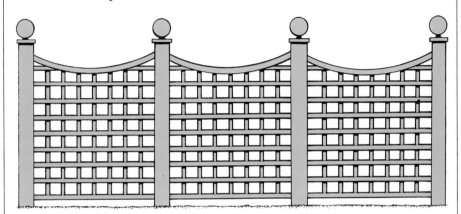

Fig. 14 Timber trellis screens painted white can be used to divide a garden. Both modern and traditional styles (shown here) are available. They make ideal supports for climbing plants.

STATUARY AND OTHER ORNAMENTS

Statuary and ornaments of various kinds, provided they are chosen and placed with care, can add the finishing touches to a garden and create 'atmosphere'.

As with paving and walling, etc, light-coloured statuary and ornaments are recommended for shady areas as they show up better than pieces in, say, lead or bronze.

Today, there is a very wide range of statues and ornaments made from reconstituted stone, in shades of white or natural-stone colours. One has a choice of complete human figures or animals and birds, busts which are best mounted on pedestals or low walls, and ornamental plant containers.

Do not overdo the use of statuary but rather use it to create focal points in the garden, to lead the eye to a particular area. A focal point can be created, say, at the end of a path, wherever a path changes direction, at the end of a lawn or in a corner of the garden.

If you use human figures or animals/birds, make sure they relate to the particular part of the garden. For instance, in a woodland setting appropriate pieces might be wood nymphs, or stone owls or squirrels. For a water feature, perhaps a human figure contemplating bathing, or stone frogs peering out of a clump of rushes. For the patio or lawn, modern or classical-style statuary or plant containers, whichever are most appropriate to the setting.

TRICKS WITH MIRRORS

If you have a dark gloomy corner formed by high walls, consider mounting a large mirror on one of the walls. This will not only reflect light and so help to lighten the corner, but will also create the illusion of depth by reflecting part of the garden. It will appear as if the garden extends beyond the wall.

The idea of using mirrors in garden design is gradually increasing in popularity as people realize how effective they can be, rather than dismissing them as mere gimmicks. Mirrors are particularly useful in very small gardens as they make the garden seem larger than it really is.

A mirror, of course, should be suited to outdoor use and this means choosing one of heavy plate glass with a waterproof back. Pre-drilled holes are essential as the mirror is fixed to a wall with brass screws, which are buffered with special plastic or rubber washers. It is likely you will have to order a mirror from a supplier specially for your situation.

A garden mirror has to be framed in some way, otherwise it will not completely create the illusion that the garden extends beyond the wall – it will simply look like the mirror hanging in the bathroom!

I would suggest ordering a mirror with an arched top, which can then be framed with false-perspective trellis. This will give the impression of an arched pathway. False-perspective trellis units are stocked by some garden centres and usually they are painted white.

There are various other ways of framing the mirror, of course. For instance, it could be surrounded by a false door frame, or a false brick or stone arch. This is presuming that the mirror is about the same height as a door – which it should be for the most effective illusion.

A very dramatic effect can be created at night by illuminating the mirror and part of the garden in front of it with low-voltage outdoor spotlights.

MAINTENANCE OF FEATURES

A problem in shady gardens, especially if conditions are also moist, is that green algae and mosses will grow on paving, paths, walls, fences, statues and other garden ornaments. This creates an unsightly green film over these features. Also, moss and algae make paved areas slippery, especially when wet.

I have this problem in my garden and have found it quite amazing how rapidly these lowly forms of plant life can spread. I have now faced the fact that I must regularly clean off paving, walls, fences and ornaments.

It is necessary to kill the moss or algae and this can be achieved by scrubbing the particular object with a masonry wash (most of which contain bleach). Alternatively you could use a horticultural algicide. It is absolutely vital that you do not allow either of these products to come into contact with cultivated plants as they will be severely damaged. Carefully follow the manufacturer's instructions on the use of these products.

Allow at least a day to elapse after applying an algicidal wash and then again scrub down the feature, using plain water. You should find that it comes up remarkably clean! The active ingredients of algicidal washes ensure that the object treated remains free from algae and moss for quite a long time. One cannot be more specific than this as algae and moss growth depends on prevailing conditions. I would recommend, though, that you treat the problem in its early stages – before it becomes well established – for the simple reason that the task is then very much quicker and easier.

Mosses and other lowly organisms, such as liverwort, growing on the soil surface (especially common in moist conditions) do not constitute a problem and certainly do not harm cultivated plants. But if you feel they are unsightly they can be controlled by regular hoeing or lightly cultivating the soil surface. This may be needed anyway to control the many other weeds that inevitably appear with monotonous regularity.

Weeds are just as much of a problem in shady areas as in sunny parts of the garden – there may be different kinds in the shady part to those in sunnier places. For instance, I have found that ground elder flourishes in shade and nettles rapidly colonize the dappled shade of my woodland.

Originally in my garden the woodland area was colonized by bracken and brambles but repeated spraying with a weedkiller containing glyphosate eradicated these horrors. Indeed, glyphosate is an extremely useful weedkiller for all perennial weeds like ground elder and nettles. Ideally it should be used when initially clearing an area for planting, although it can be used among cultivated plants such as shrubs provided you are careful not to let it drift onto their foliage, or it will kill or severely damage them. As with all weedkillers, use glyphosate strictly according to the manufacturer's instructions.

Paraquat is also a useful weedkiller for use among cultivated plants – again provided it does not come into contact with them. It is used mainly to control annual weeds, by 'burning' off the top growth.

There are weedkillers which can be applied to weedfree soil among cultivated plants to prevent the germination of weed seeds. Propachlor is one and its effect lasts for something like six to eight weeks.

Another way of preventing weed seeds from germinating is to mulch the soil around plants with bulky organic matter such as peat, pulverized bark, spent hops, spent mushroom compost (not for lime-hating plants), garden compost or well-rotted farmyard manure. Spread a layer at least 5 cm (2 in) deep over the soil surface, which must be weed-free and moist. Top up annually in the spring if necessary.

APPENDIX

SUPPLIERS OF PLANTS SUITABLE FOR SHADE

Between them, the following nurseries should be able to supply most or all of the plants recommended in this book. I suggest you send for their catalogues, which are very informative.

Beth Chatto
White Barn House
Elmstead Market
Colchester
Essex CO7 7DB
(perennials, shrubs)

Bressingham Gardens
Bressingham
Diss
Norfolk IP22 2AB
(perennials, shrubs, alpines, etc)

Broadleigh Gardens
Bishops Hull
Taunton
Somerset TA4 1AE
(bulbous plants)

P. de Jager and Sons Ltd
The Nurseries
Marden
Kent TN12 9BP
(bulbous and other plants)

Hillier Nurseries (Winchester) Ltd
Ampfield House
Ampfield
Romsey
Hampshire SO5 9PA
(shrubs, trees, climbers, perennials, etc)

Hydon Nurseries Ltd
Clock Barn Lane
Hydon Heath
Godalming
Surrey GU8 4AZ
(rhododendrons and azaleas)

W. E. Th. Ingwersen Ltd
Birch Farm Nursery
Gravetye
East Grinstead
West Sussex RH19 4LE
(alpines)

Michael Jefferson-Brown Ltd
Weston Hills
Spalding
Lincolnshire PE12 6DQ
(daffodils, lilies)

Notcutts Nurseries Ltd
Woodbridge
Suffolk IP12 4AF
(shrubs, trees, climbers, perennials, etc)

James Trehane & Sons Ltd
Camellia Nursery
Stapehill Road
Hampreston
Wimborne, Dorset BH21 7NE
(camellias)

INDEX